MONET

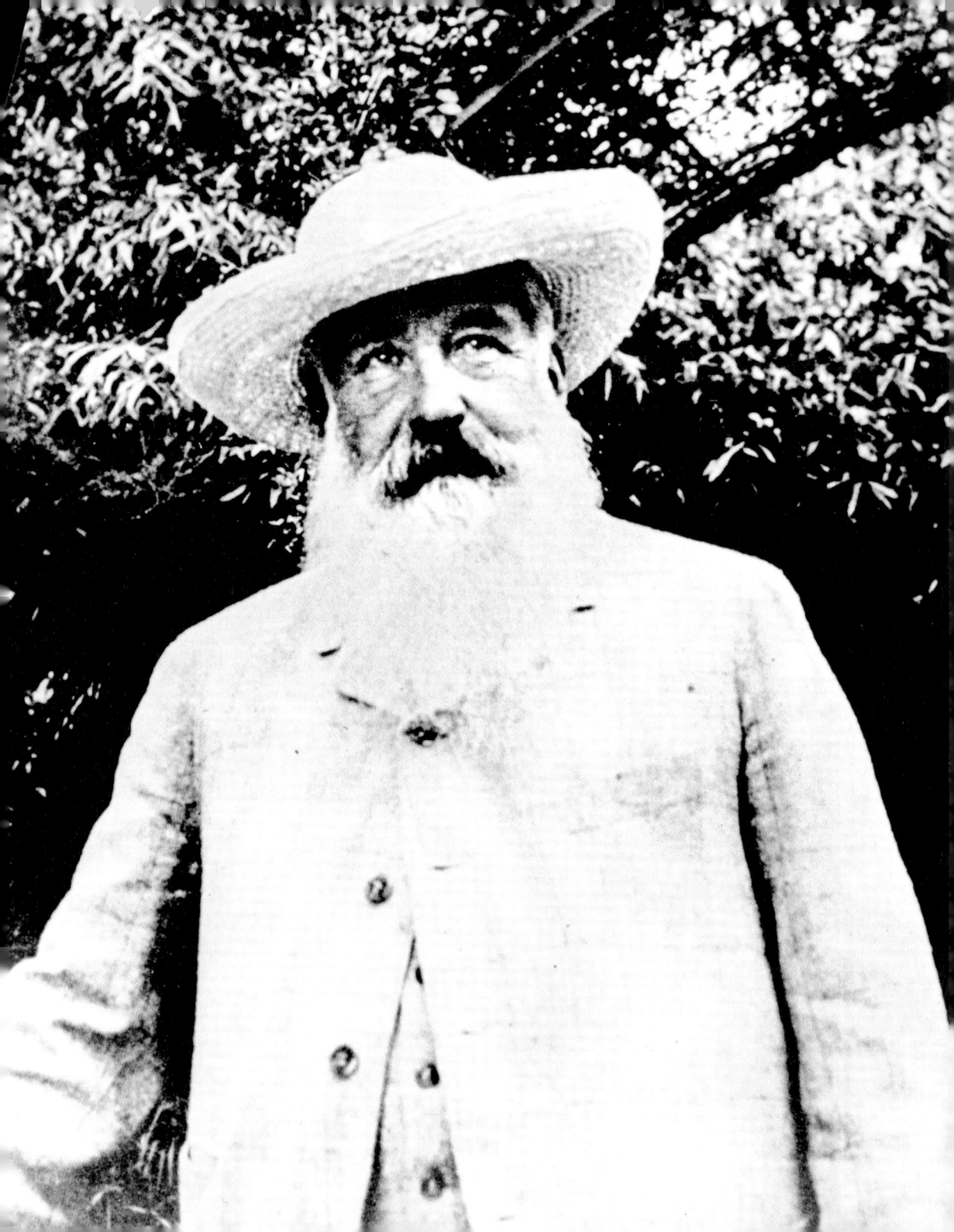

MASTERS OF ART

MONET

Rosalind Ormiston

PRESTEL

Munich · London · New York

Front Cover: Claude Monet, *Water Lilies*, 1906, The Art Institute of Chicago,
Mr. and Mrs. Martin A. Ryerson Collection
Frontispiece: Sacha Guitry, Portrait of Claude Monet at Giverny, 1915 (see page 32)
Pages 8/9: Henri Manuel, Claude Monet with his palette in front of his work
'Les Nymphéas', 1920s (see page 36)
Pages 38/39: *The Water-Lily Pond in the Evening*, 1914–22 (detail, see pages 108/09)

© Prestel Verlag, Munich · London · New York 2026
A member of Penguin Random House Verlagsgruppe GmbH
Neumarkter Strasse 28 · 81673 Munich

1st edition 2026

produktsicherheit@penguinrandomhouse.de
(The above information is mandatory information according to GPSR
and should be used for all queries relating to the safety of our books)

A CIP catalogue record for this book is available from the British Library.

Editorial direction: Cornelia Hübler, Anja Besserer
Picture editing: Fiona Krech
Copyediting and proofreading: Russell Stockman
Production management: Michael Graupner, Cilly Klotz
Design: Florian Frohnholzer, Sofarobotnik
Typesetting: Uhl + Massopust, Aalen
Separations: Reproline mediateam
Printing and binding: Livonia Print, Riga
Typeface: Cera Pro

MIX
Paper | Supporting
responsible forestry
FSC® C002795

Penguin Random House Verlagsgruppe FSC® N001967
Printed in Latvia
ISBN 978-3-7913-9379-7
www.prestel.com

CONTENTS

INTRODUCTION

The year 2024 marked the hundred and fiftieth anniversary of the designation of Impressionism in France, the art movement with which the painter Claude Monet (1840–1926) is inextricably linked. Like him, by 1874 many artists in Europe were painting outdoors, creating landscapes, streetscapes, river views and seascapes in which they sought to capture, as in a snapshot, their response to the light and colouring of a specific moment in time.

Painting outside the studio was now much simpler. Lightweight collapsible easels were readily portable, pigments now came in resealable metal tubes, and flat brushes allowed one to work with swift, broad strokes.

Monet unwittingly provided a name for this new painting approach when he gave the title *Impression, Sunrise* to a sketchlike oil he had made while watching the sun rise over the harbour of his hometown Le Havre. He happened to include it among the works he showed at a collective exhibition in the spring of 1874. Finding themselves shut out from the best opportunity for French artists to show and possibly sell their work, the highly conservative annual state-sponsored Paris Salon, a loose group of thirty artists calling itself the *Société anonyme* decided to mount a show of its own. In addition to Claude Monet, the group included such now-famous names as Paul Cézanne (1839–1906), Alfred Sisley (1839–99), Pierre-Auguste Renoir (1841–1919), Edgar Degas (1834–1917), Camille Pissarro (1830–1903), Armand Guillaumin (1841–1927) and Berthe Morisot (1841–95). For their exhibition of 165 works they rented the second-floor former atelier of photographer Nadar at 35 boulevard des Capucines.

The show opened on April 15 and ran for a month. One of its reviewers was the art critic Louis Leroy (1812–85), who, after noting the artists' attempt in so many of the works exhibited to communicate their immediate response to the scene before them, hit upon the title of Monet's *Impression* painting as a way to describe this new common style. His review published in the satirical magazine *Le Charivari* on 25 April appeared under the title "The Exhibition of the Impressionists". The show itself was poorly attended and entrance fees failed to cover the group's expenses, but the publicity generated by Leroy's and other dismissive reviews called attention to this new departure in art in the minds of the public, gallery owners and art collectors.

To many in the group the notoriety must have been a surprise. They had been painting *en plein air*, capturing typical scenes from modern life, for years. Now thanks to Leroy their painting style had a name, even though it was first used in ridicule. And they happily exploited it; they mounted a second "Impressionist" exhibition in 1876, by which time the group had been joined by the wealthy painter Gustave Caillebotte, both as exhibitor and financier. A full seven exhibitions followed the initial one, the last mounted in 1886. By that time some of the better-known artists were no longer involved, among them Monet, Sisley, Caillebotte and Renoir. They had established careers, and Impressionism had diversified, given way to new styles – the Post-impressionism of Paul Gauguin (1848–1903), Vincent van Gogh (1853–90) and Paul Cézanne and the Neo-impressionism or Pointillism introduced by Georges Seurat (1859–91) and Paul Signac (1863–1935).

Claude Monet would stay true to "Impressionism". He continued to prefer painting outdoors, letting his brush be guided by what he saw then generally finishing a work in his studio. He is known for making series of paintings of the same motif, picturing it under changing light and atmospheric conditions.

Today, more than 150 years since that groundbreaking exhibition, Impressionism is still with us. Immensely popular with museum-goers and capable of fetching astronomical prices in auction houses, it continues to inspire artists to work outdoors, to express in paint their response to the moment. And art lovers flock to the Giverny estate of one of its great exponents, Claude Monet.

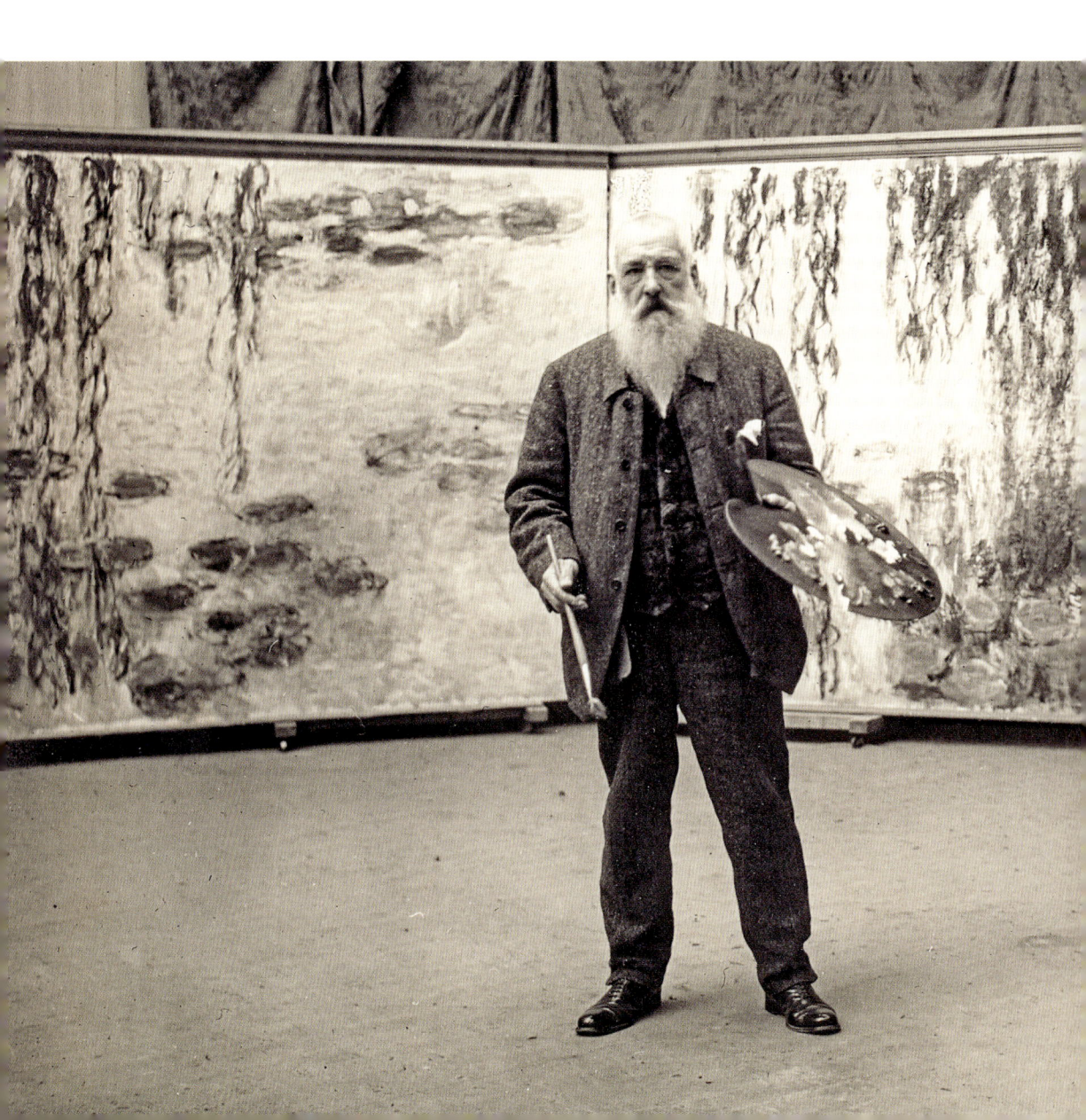

LIFE

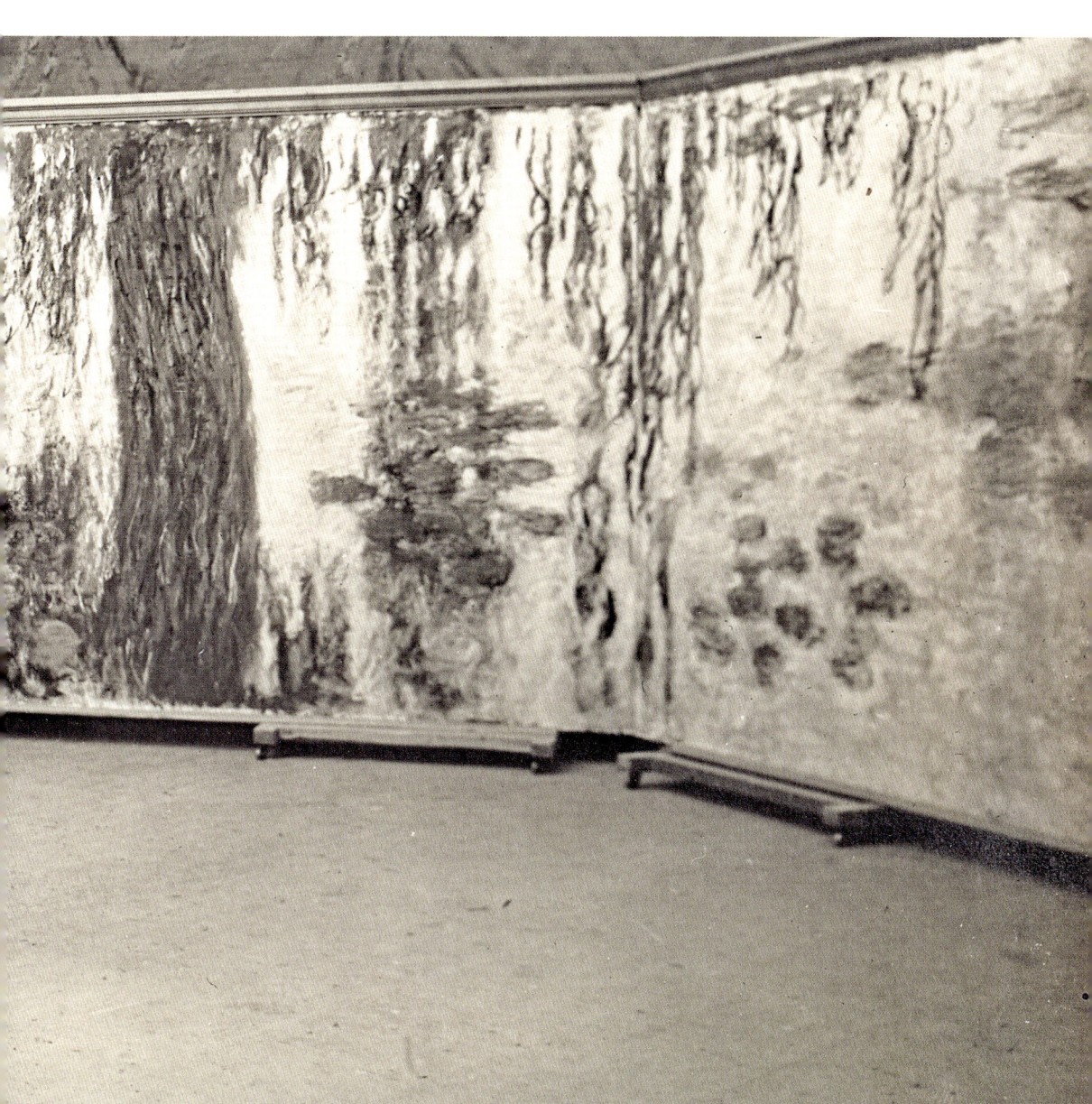

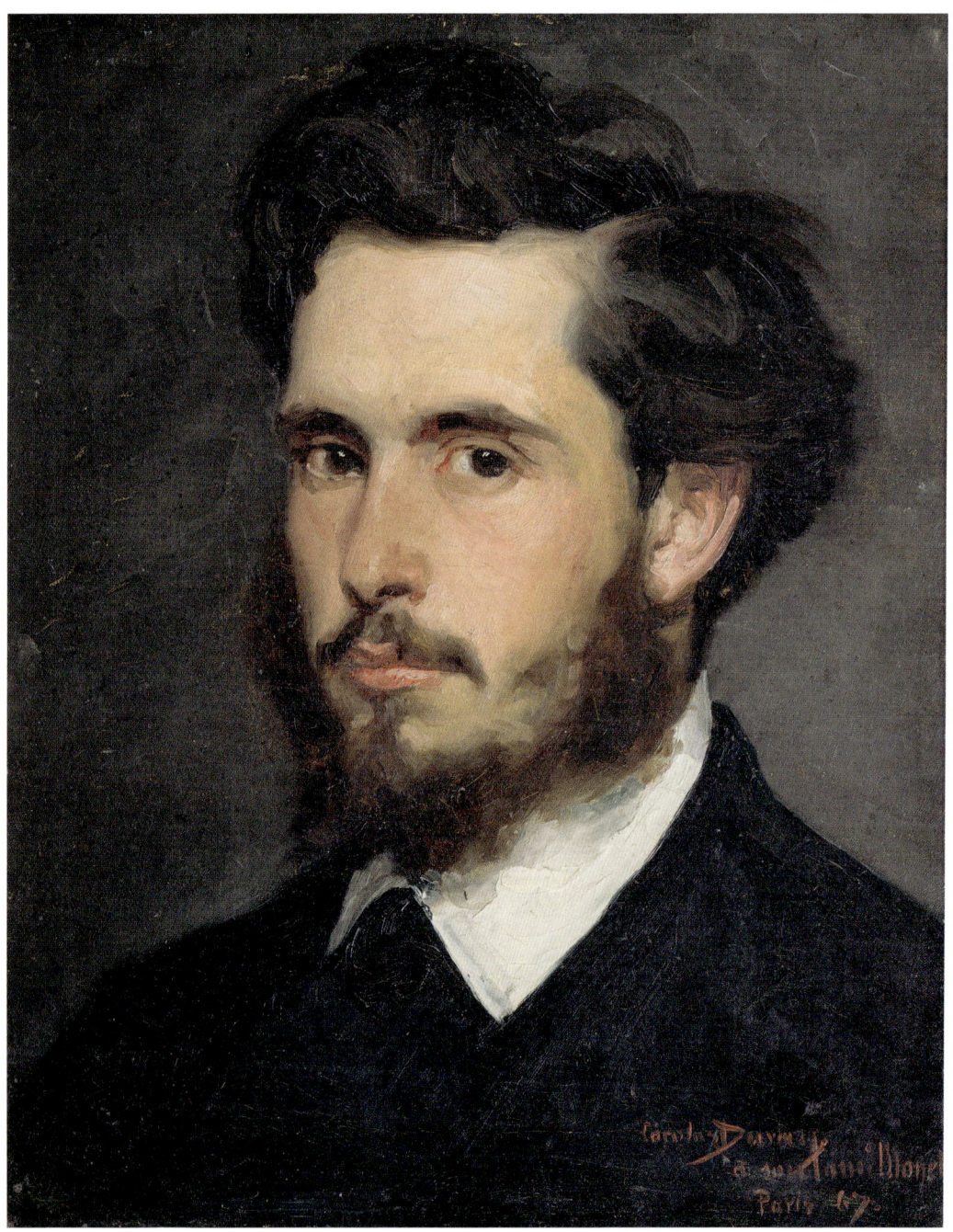

Oscar-Claude Monet (1840–1926, see page 10) was born in Paris at 45 rue Lafitte on 14 November 1840, the second son of Claude-Adolphe Monet (1800–71) and Louise-Justine Monet, née Aubrée (1805–57). His mother was thirty-five years old, childless from her first marriage but now with two children by her second husband Claude-Adolphe, aged forty.

In 1845 the couple moved with sons Leon Pascal (1836–1917) and Oscar – as he was called – to the port city Le Havre in northwest France, where they occupied a house, in the suburb Ingouville, large enough for them to take in boarders. Claude-Adolphe worked close by as a ship's chandler in a wholesale business owned by Jacques Lecadre, the husband of his half-sister Marie-Jeanne, née Gaillard (b. 1790). Lecadre was a "wholesale grocer and supplier of ships' provisions". He and his wife were prosperous and notable members of the community, which now included the Monet family. The Lecadres owned a country house in Sainte-Adresse, a fishing village. The location would later feature in Monet's paintings.

Monet's early interest in art was encouraged by his mother but less so by his father, who wanted him to pursue a business career. On the death of his mother in 1857 Monet moved with his father and brother to the nearby residence of his childless aunt Marie-Jeanne Lacadre. For Monet it was especially fortunate because Marie-Jeanne was an amateur artist with her own studio. She knew the artist Amand Gautier (1825–94) and his circle of painters. Marie-Jeanne encouraged Monet to continue his art studies. In 1851, aged ten, he entered the "collège communal" in Le Havre, receiving instruction in Latin and Greek. At the college he took drawing lessons from Jacques-François Ochard (1800–70), a former student of the noted Neoclassical painter Jacques-Louis David (1748–1825). Ochard taught in the academic tradition with life-drawing from plaster casts.

Local Caricatures

Monet's early drawings from this period included harbour scenes, studies of local buildings and boats, and excellent caricatures of local residents. The caricature drawings were popular among his friends and Monet sold them at varying prices, reaching a peak of twenty francs. In total he would earn 2,000 francs from the drawings. He had a knack for capturing the physiology of different faces. Some of the drawings were displayed locally in the windows of the Gravier stationer's shop in Le Havre that sold art supplies and ironmongery. The drawings were spotted by artist Eugène Boudin (1824–98, see pages 12/13), a friend of Ochard's living in Le Havre and possibly joint-owner of the shop. A meeting between Boudin and Monet resulted in the older man's agreeing to mentor Monet, who was a better draughtsman than painter.

At this time it can be seen that Monet's eventual path toward a painting career had begun. He admitted later in life that he had been disruptive at school, rebellious, eager to bend rules. He preferred to be outdoors. Now he would learn from Boudin, a marine and landscape painter and one of the first artists to paint outdoors – *en plein air*.

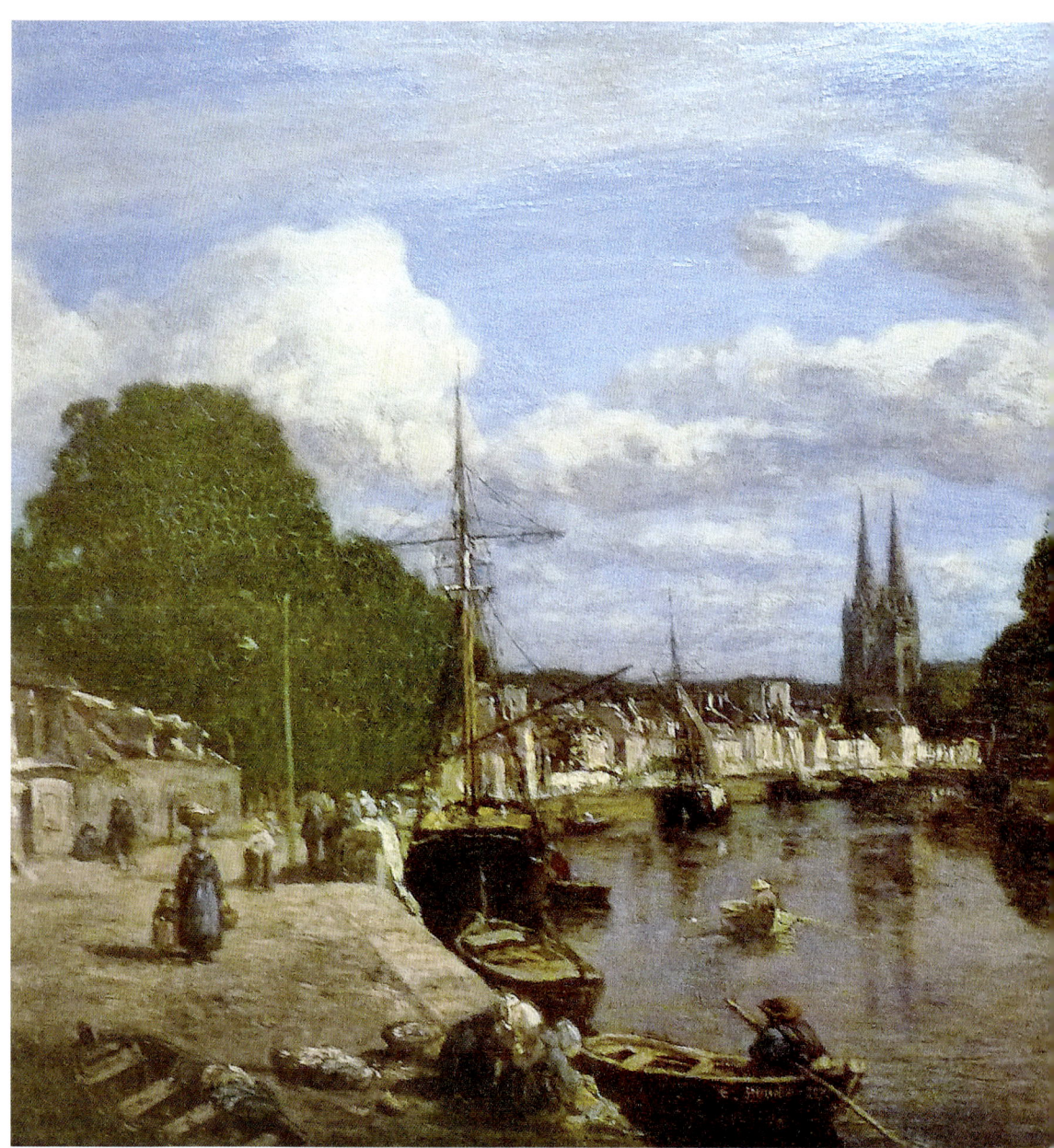

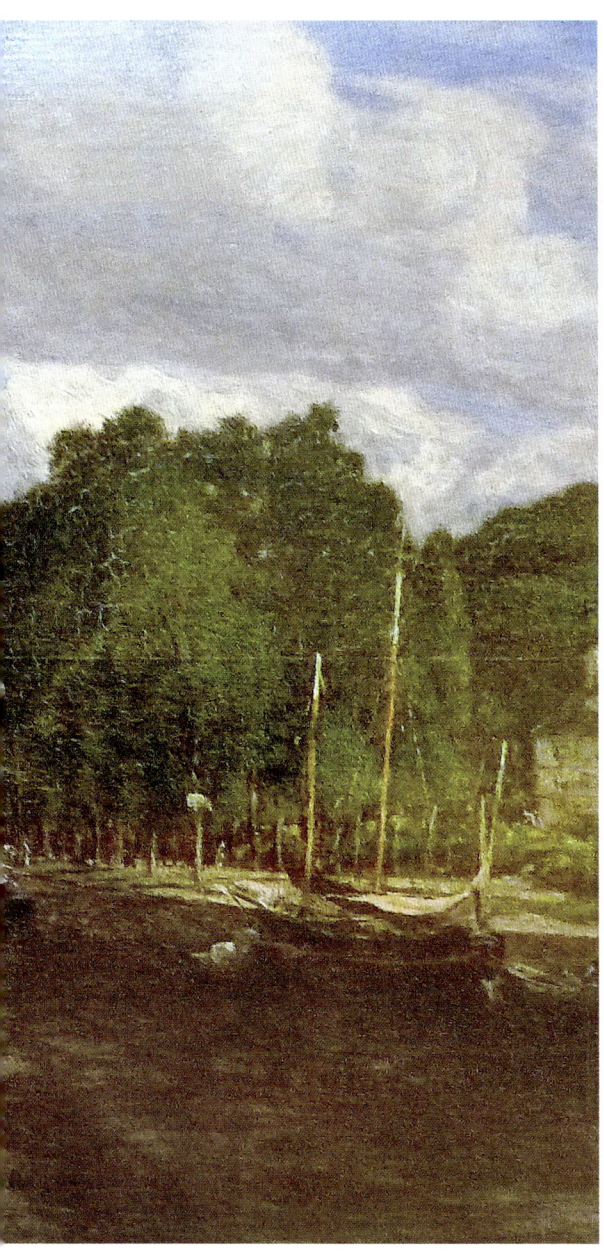

Eugène Boudin, *The Port at Quimper*, 1857,
Musée des Beaux-Arts de Quimper

He also encouraged Monet to sketch, draw and paint in the open air, direct from nature, and abandon the caricatures. Together they painted in different locations in Honfleur and Trouville and in and around Le Havre. From this experience Monet learned to paint landscapes and marine scenes. His later recollection of his time with Boudin, studying, drawing and painting, was that "it was as if a veil suddenly lifted from my eyes and I knew that I could be a painter." The differences between their approaches was that Boudin included many figures in his landscapes. Monet began to as well, but eventually phased out figures in order to concentrate on the atmosphere at different times of day, in changing light and shadow.

First Exhibition

When Monet was not yet eighteen the Société des Amis des Arts in Le Havre gave him a first chance to exhibit his work. During August and September 1858 his recent painting *View at Rouelles* (page 41) was displayed. He applied for an art scholarship to be sponsored by the city of Le Havre but was unsuccessful. His father, although concerned about his son's choice of an art career, wanted him to succeed. Monet persevered and managed to enrol at the Académie Suisse in Paris, a walk-in studio school. There he met Camille Pissarro (1830–1903) a Danish-French painter born on St Thomas (now U.S. Virgin Islands) then living in Paris. They would become great friends. Pissarro, ten years older than Monet, was always willing to offer advice and

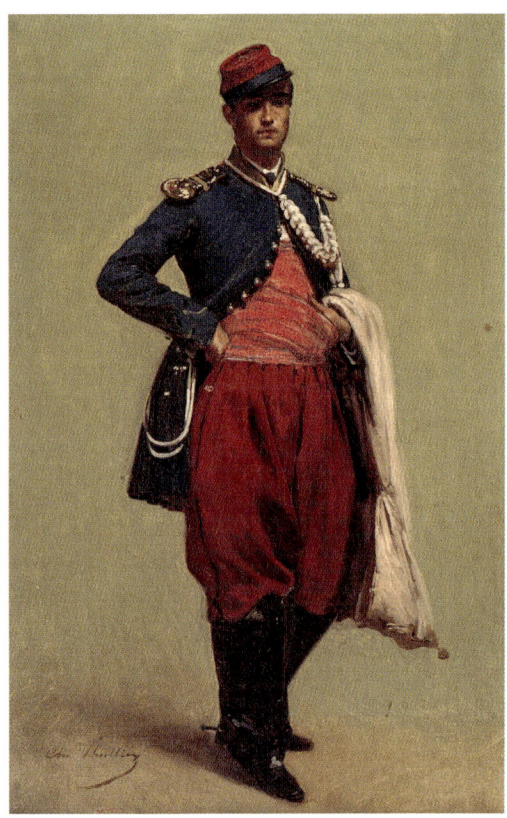

Charles-Marie Lhuillier, *Portrait of Claude Monet in Uniform*, 1861, Musée Marmottan Monet, Paris

Algeria

The following summer Monet became ill while on active service, contracting typhoid fever that lasted many weeks. After two months' convalescence in Algeria he was sent home to France to recuperate. It was at this time, around October 1862, that he met the Dutch landscape painter Johan Barthold Jongkind (1819–91), who was staying in Le Havre. Monet would be informally mentored by Jongkind, whom he recalled as "a quiet man with such a talent that is beyond words." Monet went even further: "From that moment on he was my true master, and it is to him that I owe the real education of my eye." The combined mentorship of Boudin and Jongkind proved formative for Monet's future focus as a landscape painter. By November Monet was demobilised with the help of his aunt Lecadre, who paid the military around 3,000 francs to have another recruit take Monet's place. She wanted her nephew to continue his artistic education in Paris, mentored by the painter Auguste Toulmouche (1829–90), who had meanwhile married into the family.

The aspiring young artist was known to be a rebel, with no grasp of finances. He routinely failed to pay his rent, was chased by bailiffs, and settled other unpaid bills with paintings. Monet had accumulated money from his caricature drawings and received an allowance from his father to pay for his studies and rent, but his aunt and his father threatened to withdraw support unless he socialised less and studied more. Toulmouche recommended that Monet join the atelier of the Swiss-

introduce the younger man to his contacts. Meanwhile, in Le Havre Monet's widowed 60-year-old father acknowledged the birth of an illegitimate daughter, Marie Monet (1860–91), born to Armande Célestine Vatine (b. 1836), his 24-year-old domestic servant. (He did not tell his sister Marie-Jeanne or his sons.) That same year Claude-Adolphe retired from the Lecadre firm. In March 1861 his son Claude Monet received, like many young Frenchmen, his call-up papers for seven years' military service. Three months later Monet was in Algeria, mobilised with the First Regiment of African Light Cavalry (see above).

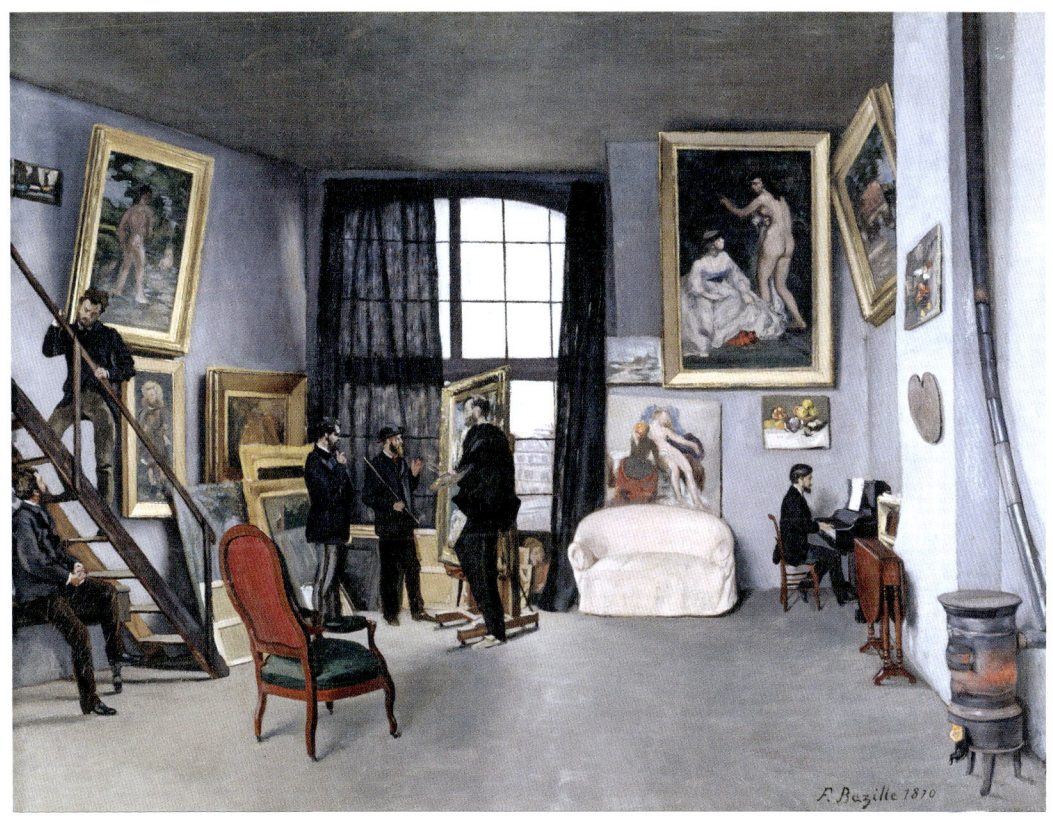

Frédéric Bazille, *L'Atelier de Bazille, 9 rue de la Condamine in Paris*, 1870, Musée d'Orsay, Paris

born academic history painter Charles Gleyre (1806–74). In his time Gleyre taught many artists who would become key contributors to Impressionism in France; Alfred Sisley (1839–99), Jean-Frédéric Bazille (1841–70), Pierre-Auguste Renoir (1841–1919) and Monet were among them. Bazille came from a wealthy wine production family in Montpellier and could afford a permanent studio in Paris (see above). He let Renoir and Monet, both often penniless, stay in it and use it for work. All four would remain friends, exchanging ideas, exhibiting together, often painting each other's portraits (see page 16). One example is Renoir's *Monet Painting in his Garden in Argenteuil*, 1873 (Wadsworth Atheneum, Hartford).

Realism

In 1849/50 the French painter Gustave Courbet (1819–77) created the monumental work *Burial at Ornans* (Musée d'Orsay, Paris). It was a work of realism, recording participants at a provincial funeral in his native Ornans, a village in the Franche-Comté in eastern France. Courbet's art was informed by his visit to Holland and Belgium in 1846/47, noting

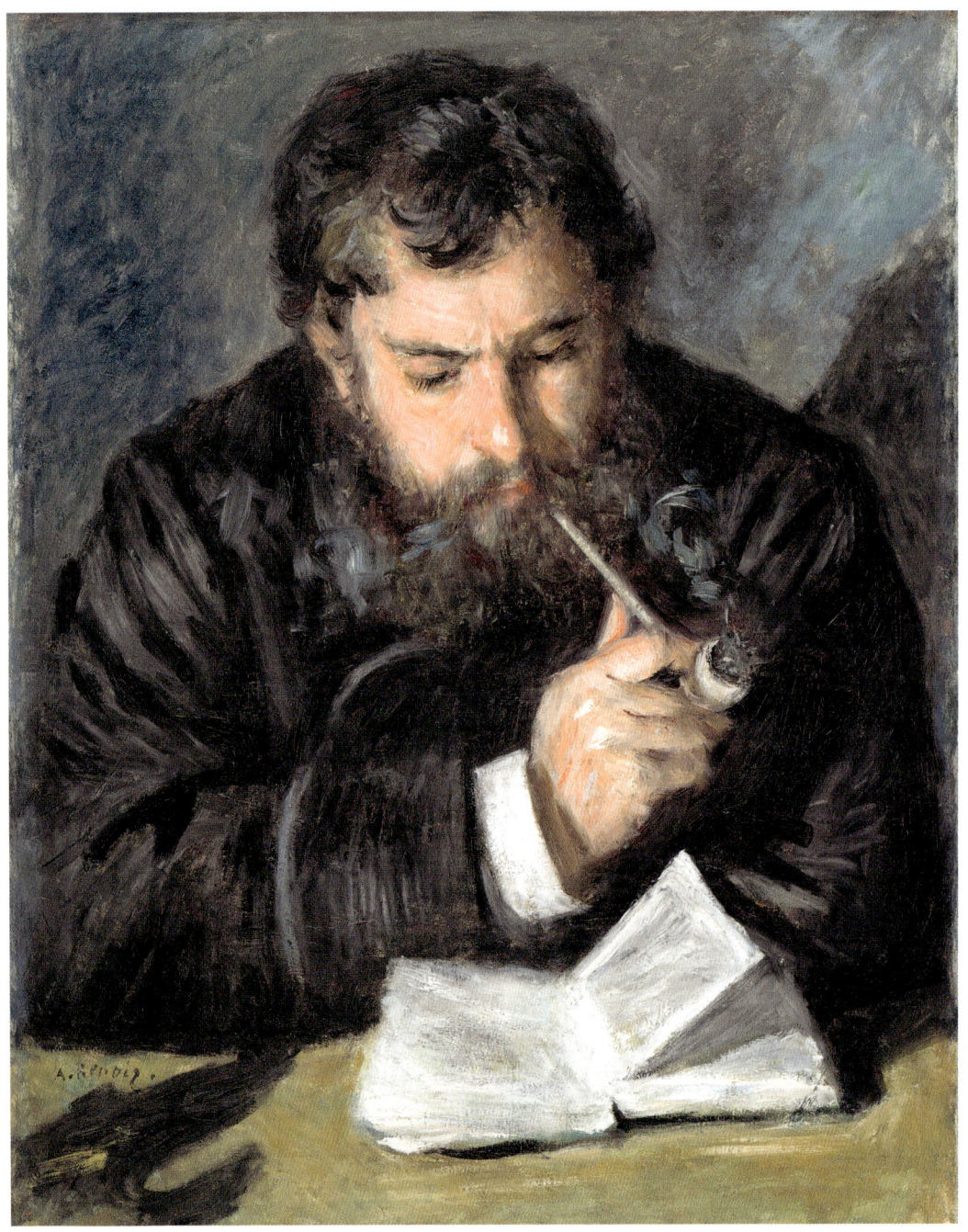

the realism in artworks by Dutch and Belgian painters portraying real people in everyday settings. Courbet's work, vast in size, was exhibited at the 1850/51 Paris Salon. The presention of ordinary people in a painting of a size reserved for scenes from history was savaged by critics. Courbet shrugged off the criticism. His opinion was that *A Burial at Ornans* was in reality the burial of an art movement, Romanticism replaced by realism. For many art historians this work marks a setting out in a completely new direction, with artists rejecting academic conventions, moving away from the control held by the official art academies in France in order to paint everyday life. And more "isms" – different art methods and styles – would flourish. Seven years after the furore created by Courbet's controversial work Monet set out to become a professional painter. He too would receive savage criticism for some of his work termed "Impressionism". It was a last-gasp attack by the establishment – the Académie des Beaux-Arts and the archaic hierarchy controlling the annual Paris Salon.

The Roots of Modernity in Paris

Courbet was not alone; the art of Jean-François Millet (1814–75) also focused on the peasant poor. But it was the restructuring of Paris with urban modernism instigated by Emperor Napoleon III and organised by Georges-Eugène Haussmann (Prefect of the Seine), known as the "Haussmannisation of the city", that ushered in the new. Medieval-era rabbit-warren streets were replaced with wide boulevards and open spaces for parks. Consolidation of its railway infrastructure increased Paris's population, commerce and prosperity. (A Paris–Le Havre railway line opened in 1847, which Monet regularly used while studying in Paris.) Artists in Paris set out to paint contemporary life *en plein air*, often taking day-return journeys along the Seine to Asnières and Argenteuil, a train ride of fifteen minutes from the Gare St-Lazare. They painted "impressions" of the railway station too. One writer who recorded this new way of living was the French art critic Charles Baudelaire (1821–67). His book *Le Peintre de la Vie Moderne* (*The Painter of Modern Life*) was published in 1863. He defined modernity as "the transient, the fleeting" – different from the past.

Monet and Bazille

Following his penchant for the outdoors, Monet spent the spring of 1863 with Frédéric Bazille in Chailly-en-Bière, a village close to Barbizon near the forest of Fontainebleau south of Paris. Monet returned there in 1864; both summers were spent in Le Havre and Sainte-Adresse, and Saint-Siméon near Honfleur, close to home. Gleyre's studio had been forced to close in July 1864 for lack of funds. In 1865 Monet stayed in Chailly-en-Bière again with Bazille while working on a preliminary painting, *The Luncheon on the Grass* (Pushkin State Museum, Moscow, page 45), in preparation for a larger-scale version of the composition. It was a response to Édouard Manet's controversial painting *The Luncheon on the*

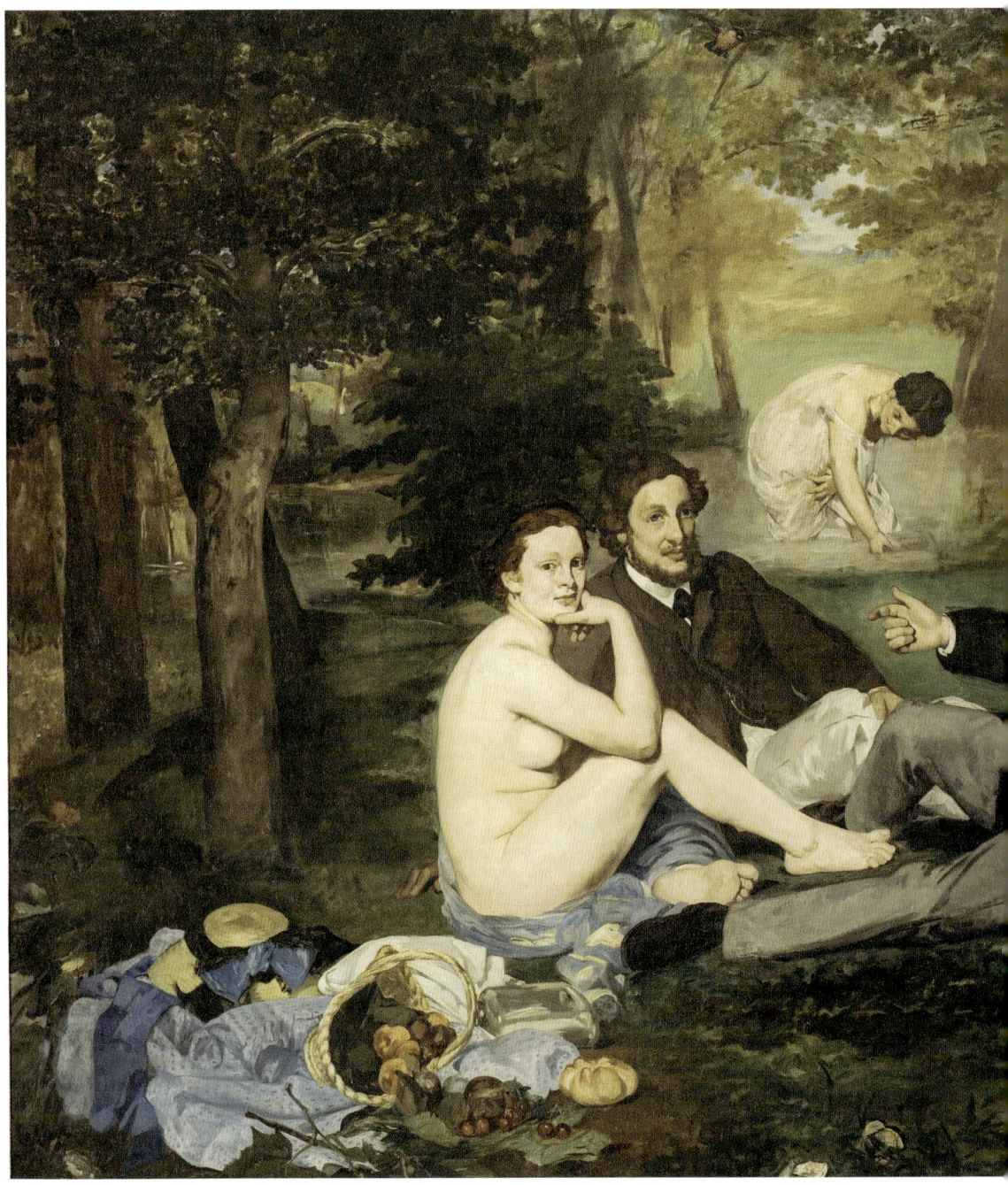

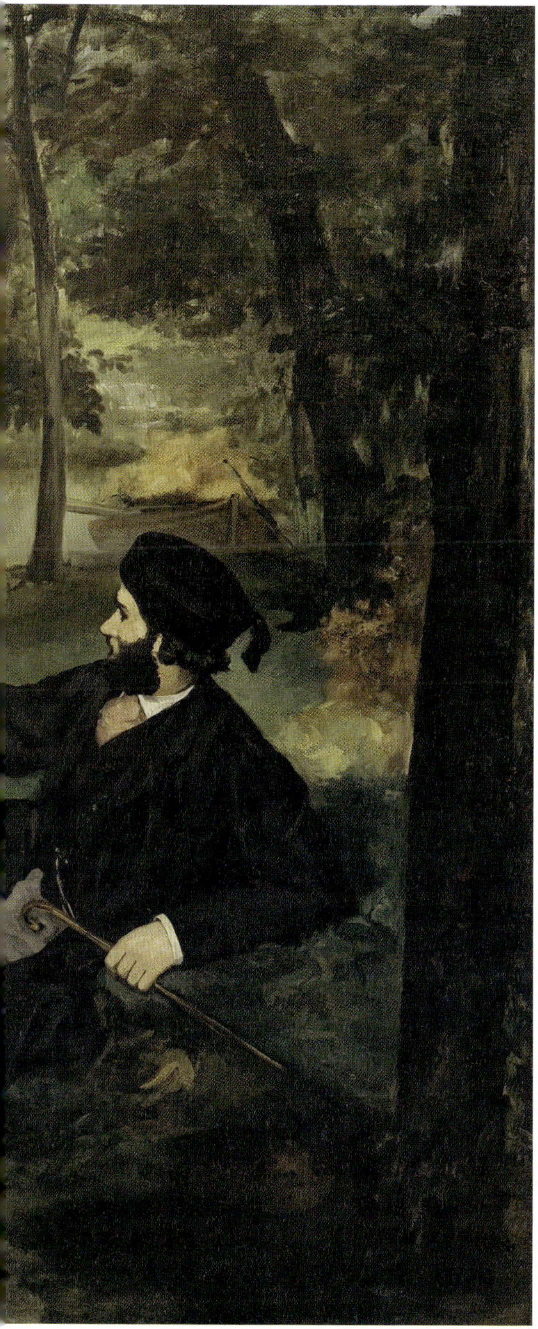

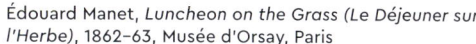

Édouard Manet, *Luncheon on the Grass (Le Déjeuner sur l'Herbe)*, 1862–63, Musée d'Orsay, Paris

Grass,1863 (Musée d'Orsay, Paris, see pages 18/19), also called *The Bath*. Bazille and Camille Doncieux (1847–79), Monet's model and girlfriend, posed for the figures depicted in a preliminary study, *Bazille and Camille* (*Study for Luncheon on the Grass*), 1865 (National Gallery of Art, Washington).

Claude and Camille

Monet first exhibited at the Paris Salon in 1865. (His work would be accepted again in 1866, 1868, and 1880.) 1865 was also the year in which Monet met Camille Léonie Doncieux in Paris. Camille, originally from Lyon, was born on 15 January 1847, the first daughter of Claude Charles Doncieux, a *negociant* (salesman), and Léonie Doncieux, née Manechalle. The family had moved to Paris during Camille's childhood. Around eighteen years of age, Camille worked as a model, posing for Renoir and Manet among others. She would become Monet's favourite model, his muse, his lover and wife. During their life together Camille would be depicted in more than fifty Monet paintings, often posing as more than one figure. For the remarkable large-scale *Luncheon on the Grass*, 1865/66 (Musée d'Orsay, Paris) she posed as all five women. The painting was not finished in time for the annual Salon. It was stored but deteriorated owing to damp conditions. Monet cut out the damaged areas and two sections remain.

At the Salon he showed two marine paintings, *La Pointe de la Hève at Low Tide* (Kimbell Art Museum, Fort Worth, page 43), and its pendant *The Mouth of the Seine at Honfleur* (Norton Simon

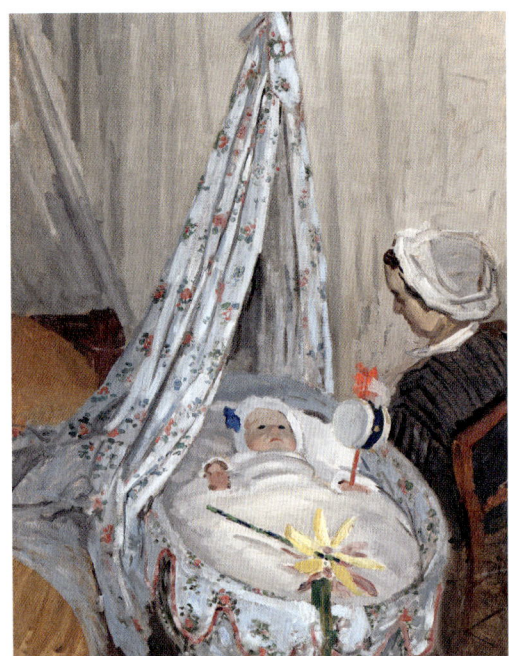

Claude Monet, *The Cradle, Camille with the Artist's Son Jean*, 1867, National Gallery of Art, Washington, Collection of Mr. and Mrs. Paul Mellon

Museum, Pasadena), which pictured the choppy waters where the Seine river meets the English Channel. Both were sketched on site and finished in his studio. His work acknowledged the realism of Courbet yet met the standards of the academic Salon and received critical praise. However, it was another work, *Camille* or *The Woman in the Green Dress*, 1866 (Kunsthalle, Bremen, page 49), that captured attention and won Monet a silver medal.

Sainte-Adresse

Following his initial success at the Salon, where he sold his works, Monet and Camille stayed in Honfleur, where he painted a series of snow scenes during the winter months. In April 1867 Monet painted

alongside Renoir in Paris. Camille was pregnant. In need of income, Monet chose to leave her in Paris and stay with his family in Le Havre, possibly in order to show them that he was creating saleable works. He worked feverishly on twenty canvases featuring family scenes and local views. *Woman in the Garden, Sainte-Adresse* (State Hermitage Museum, St Petersburg) depicts part of the landscaped garden of the Coteau estate at Sainte-Adresse, which belonged to Monet's cousin Paul-Eugene Lecadre. The painting features Lecadre's wife Marguerite standing close to a raised bed, a *corbeille* with single-colour planting. She wears fashionable clothes and carries a small parasol. The painting captures Monet's impression of the fleeting effect of sunlight on the landscaped garden painted directly from nature. He included his father in *Adolphe Monet in the Garden of Le Coteau at Sainte-Adresse*. His approach is different in *The Beach of Sainte Adresse* (The Art Institute of Chicago), where the focus is on the effect of dull light from a clouded sky on the sea and shingle beach. Here he used monotone colours to capture light and atmosphere in contrast to the bright colours of the garden scenes.

Birth of Jean Monet (1867–1914)

As a pregnant woman carrying an illegitimate child, Camille was not invited to Le Havre. Her parents were dismayed that she was pregnant. Monet's father would not give him money to support

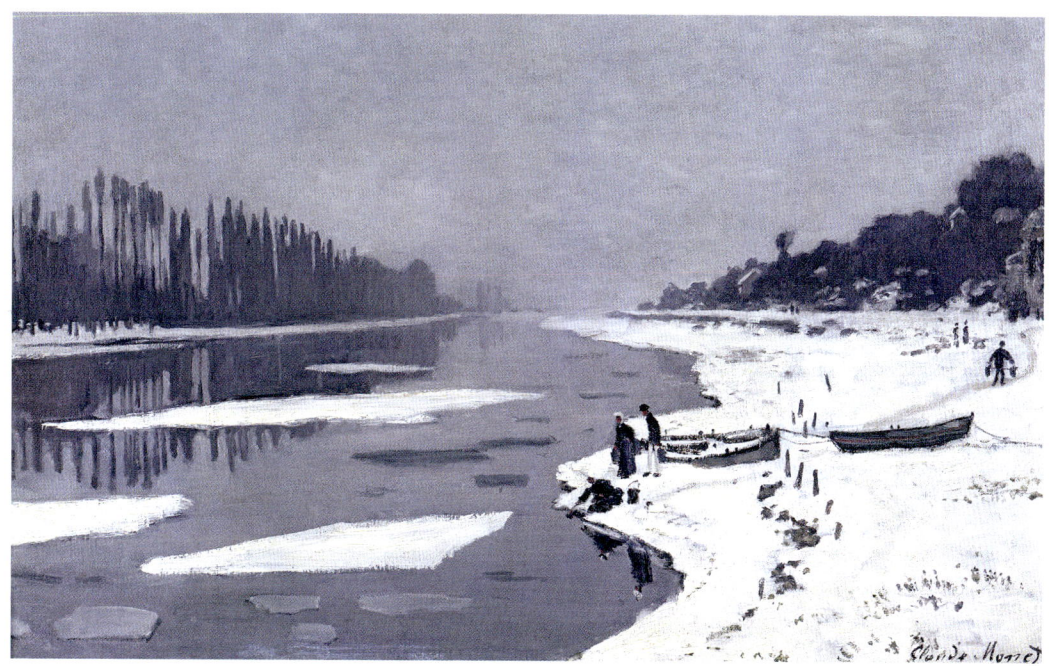

Claude Monet, *Ice Floes on the Seine at Bougival*, ca. 1867, Musée d'Orsay, Paris

or even visit her. French law did not allow young people to marry without parental consent. Monet wrote letters to his wealthy friend Frédéric Bazille begging to borrow money to help Camille. On Jean's birth on 8 August 1867 Monet accepted official responsibility as the baby's father and Bazille became the infant's godfather. For Monet, an atheist, the infant's baptism was one of the rare times he took part in a church service. Over the following months Monet spent more time with Camille and Jean. He created many paintings of his son, including *The Cradle, Camille with the Artist's Son Jean*, 1867 (National Gallery of Art, Washington, see page 20), a family snapshot. Some sources say that the seated woman was Julie Vellay, Jean's godmother and the partner of Camille Pissarro. After a letter to Bazille pleading poverty, Monet was able to use a new studio his friend had ac-

quired at 9 Rue de la Paix in Paris and Bazille found a buyer for one of Monet's works. In winter he went to Bougival, west of Paris, to picture the ice on the river, as in *Ice Floes on the Seine at Bougival*, ca. 1867, a near-monochrome work capturing the intensity of the ice-white snow and near-purple reflection of the water. He needed to make money, but his style of painting had not changed (see above).

Les Batignolles

In the 1860s and '70s a regular meeting place for artists on Thursdays and Sundays was the Café Guerbois on Place de Clichy. Here Monet, Manet, Cézanne, Pissarro, Bazille, Renoir and others would gather if they were in Paris. Manet and Degas were

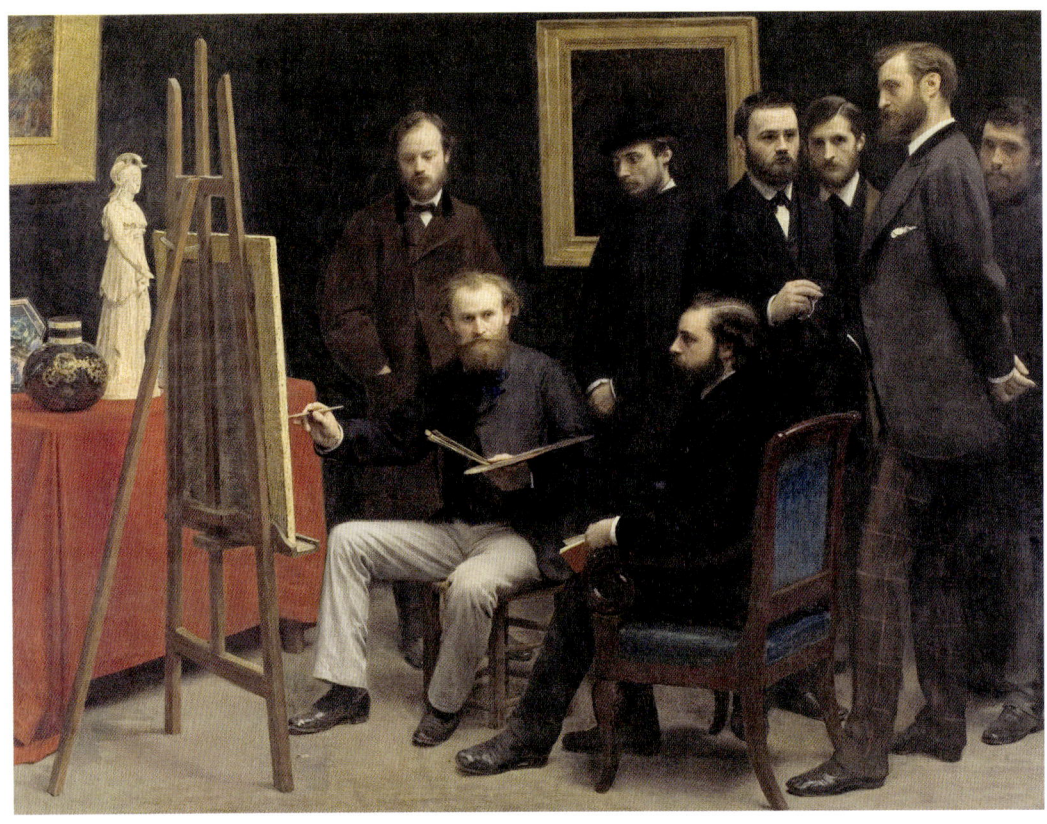

Henri Fantin-Latour, *Studio at Les Batignolles*, 1870, Musée d'Orsay, Paris

among the studio painters, while Monet, Cézanne, Pissarro, Bazille and Sisley favoured *en-plein-air* work; Renoir liked both strategies. Led by Manet, they were known as the Batignolles group, after the district they lived in. Henri Fantin-Latour painted a group portrait, *Studio at Les Batignolles*, 1870 (Musée d'Orsay, Paris, see above). The communal gathering created strong bonds and a determination to sell work outside the Paris Salon. The outdoor artists often painted together. In 1869 Monet and Renoir had painted the same scenes at La Grenouillère (the Frog Pond) on the Seine west of Paris, works that are considered among their Im-

pressionist masterpieces. Renoir's *La Grenouillère* (Nationalmuseum, Stockholm) and *La Grenouillère* (Oskar Reinhart Collection, Winterthur) focus on the people – bathing, chatting, enjoying a social get-together on the "Camembert", a round floating platform with the floating restaurant just in focus. Monet's *La Grenouillère* (The Metropolitan Museum of Art, New York, see page 23) and *Bathers at La Grenouillère* (The National Gallery, London) also pictured the Camembert, people swimming, the rowboats for hire and the plank leading to the floating restaurant, but his primary focus was on the riverscape and the effect of dappled sunlight

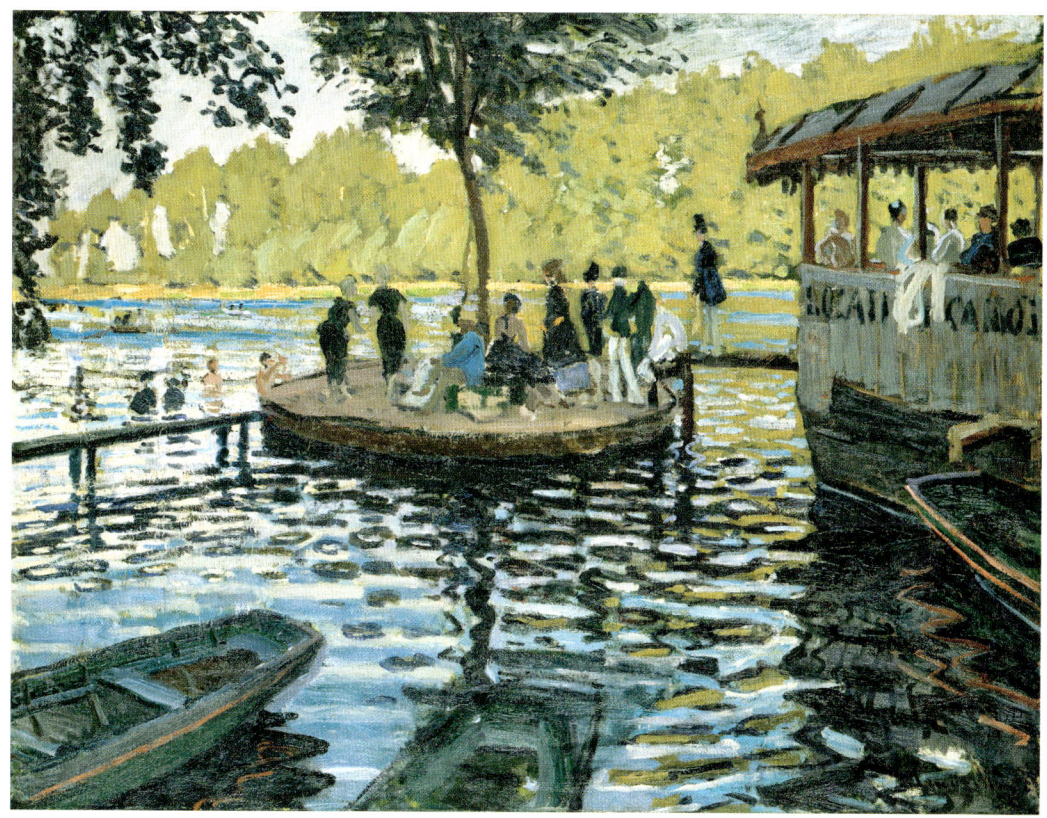

Claude Monet, *La Grenouillère*, 1869, The Metropolitan Museum of Art, New York, Collection of Mr. and Mrs. Paul Mellon

and shadow on the water. Today the paintings they produced are near-priceless, but at the time Monet wrote to Bazille in despair: "For eight days no bread, no wine, no fire, no light. It's atrocious!"

Franco-Prussian War 1870/71

Camille and Monet were married on 28 June 1870. His aunt Marie-Jeanne Lacadre was too ill to attend and died a few days later on 7 July. (His father Claude-Adolphe and Armande Vatine mar-

ried that same year on 31 October.) The following months of July and August were spent on a working holiday in the resort town Trouville-sur-Mer on the Normandy coast, staying at the inexpensive Hôtel Tivoli. Camille was Monet's model for a series of paintings produced here, including *Camille on the Beach in Trouville* (page 59). His love of architecture appears regularly as part of a scene, as in *The Beach at Trouville* (Wadsworth Atheneum, Hartford). By the autumn of 1870 many Parisians, including Monet, Pissarro and other artists, had left Paris to flee fighting during the Franco-Prussian War. Monet's great friend Frédéric Bazille stayed

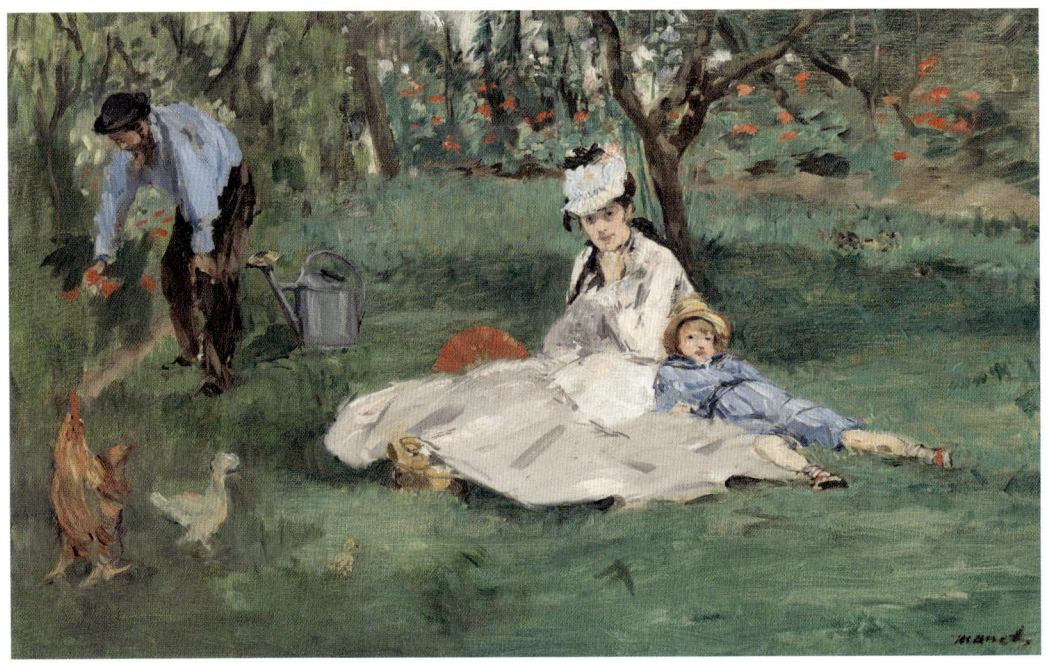

Édouard Manet, *The Monet Family in Their Garden at Argenteuil*, 1874, The Metropolitan Museum of Art, New York, Bequest of Joan Whitney Payson, 1975

and joined a regiment in August. He was killed on the battlefield on 28 November.

Monet travelled to England, settling in London, and Camille arrived soon afterward. Without much money, they lived inexpensively in the Holborn area, moving to Kensington in January 1871. Monet visited the museums and galleries, taking time to study the paintings of J.M.W. Turner (1775–1851) in the National Gallery and in South Kensington. Turner's paintings often included as a focal point a small ball of orange-red for the sun setting or rising, much like the dash of red paint in landscape paintings by the English artist John Constable (1776–1837). This would later appear in Monet's marine paintings, notably *Impression, Sunrise*, 1872 (Musée Marmottan Monet, Paris). Monet acknowledged his admiration for the English painter but did not refer to Turner's work as an influence on him. During the months

he spent in England Monet and Pissarro, who was staying in a suburb of London, would get together to paint. One of Monet's views was *The Thames Below Westminster*, ca. 1871 (The National Gallery, London). Another was *Green Park, London*, 1870/71 (Philadelphia Museum of Art). Yet he produced only seven paintings during his nine-month stay.

The artist Charles-François Daubigny (1817–78), also in London, introduced Monet and Pissarro to the French art dealer Paul Durand-Ruel (1831–1922), who had been staying in the capital since September 1870. It was a fortuitous meeting; Durand-Ruel loved their work, immediately purchasing two works by Monet. He had organised an exhibition of French art shipped from Paris. The first exhibition of the Society of French Artists was presented at the German Gallery at 168 New Bond Street in central London. Back in France, Pissarro and Monet introduced Durand-Ruel to their artist friends including Renoir, Manet and Sisley. Monet later attested that without Durand-Ruel he would never have survived as an artist. By the time of the art dealer's death in 1922 he had purchased more than 1,500 works by Renoir, 1,000 by Monet and around 800 by Pissarro.

Growing Recognition

With the Franco-Prussian War ended Monet headed back to France with his family by way of the Netherlands, where they stayed in Zaandam, just north of Amsterdam. There he created atmospheric visions like *Windmill and Boats near Zaandam, Holland*, 1871 (Ny Carlsberg Glyptotek, Copenhagen). Over the years Monet would paint more than a thousand works featuring water.

Returned to France, they lived in Argenteuil for nearly seven years. With greater financial security thanks to Durand-Ruel, Monet kept a studio in Paris as well. His painting *The Artist's House at Argenteuil*, 1873 (The Art Institute of Chicago) provides a sense of its relaxed ambience and includes Camille looking out from a door and Jean playing with a hoop. Monet's circumstances had clearly improved. Later in 1875 Durand-Ruel stopped buying Impressionist works until 1880, so Monet relied on various other art dealers. It would take some time for the general public to accept the Impressionist avant-garde.

Many of the group members' paintings from this period picture their colleagues outdoors in

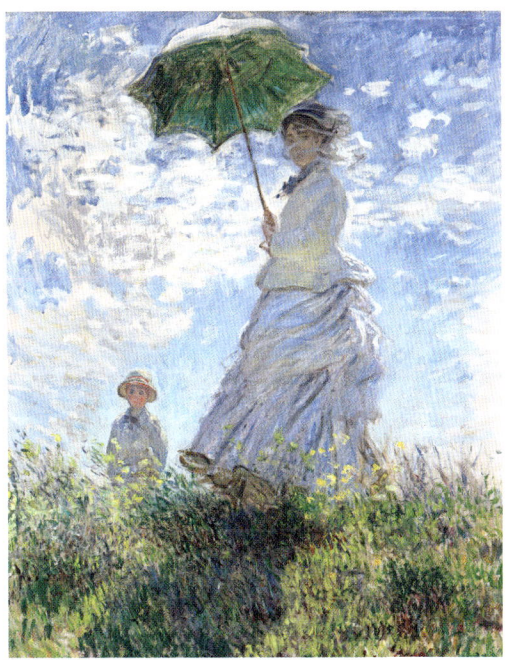

Claude Monet, *Woman with a Parasol – Madame Monet and Her Son*, 1875, National Gallery of Art, Washington, Collection of Mr. and Mrs. Paul Mellon

informal domestic scenes. In Manet's *The Monet Family in Their Garden at Argenteuil*, 1874 (The Metropolitan Museum of Art, New York, see page 24), for example, Monet, Camille and Jean are pictured at home with their chickens. On one of his visits Renoir painted the same setting in *Madame Monet and Her Son*, 1874 (National Gallery of Art, Washington). Renoir painted a superb portrait of Monet with palette in hand in *Portrait of the Painter Claude Monet*, 1875 (Musée d'Orsay, Paris). Monet painted Camille and Jean from a low angle in *Woman with a Parasol – Madame Monet and Her Son*, 1875 (National Gallery of Art, Washington, see above). She has just turned toward the painter, and her skirt is still swirling about her. Monet had the eye of a camera, and here captured a split second of time as she walked under the hot sun.

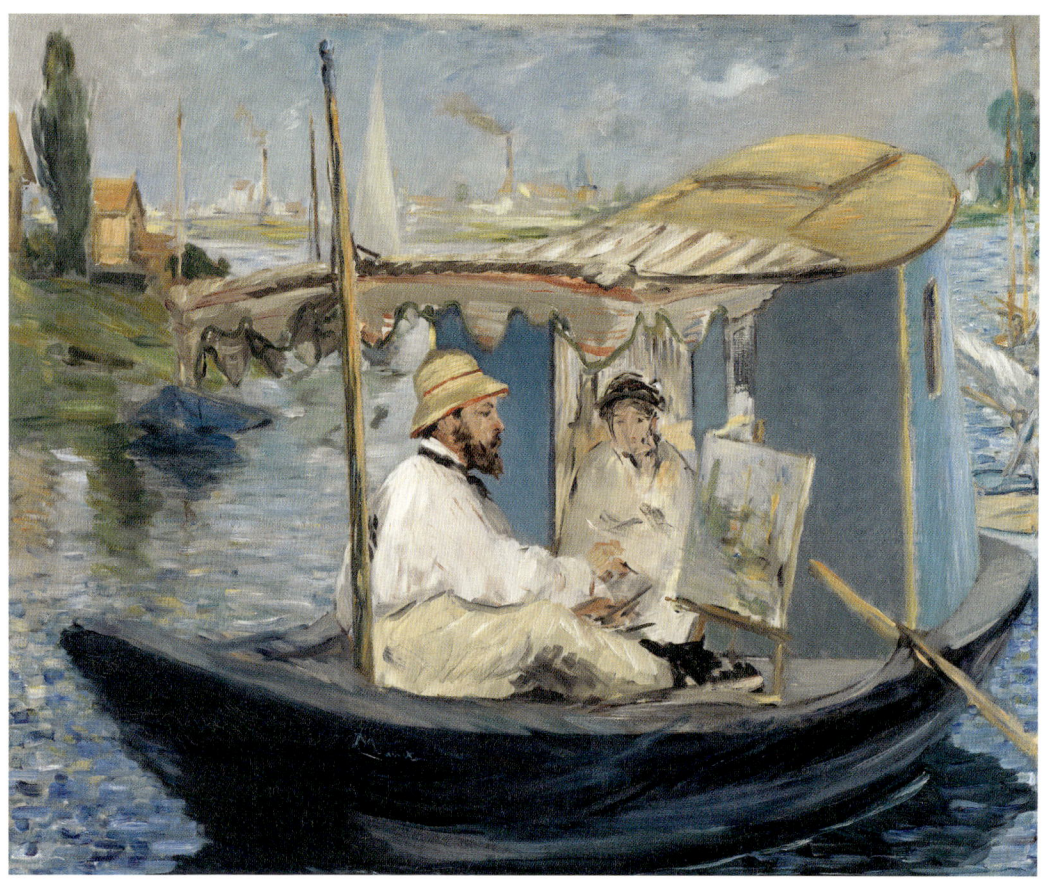

Édouard Manet, *Claude Monet Painting in His Studio Boat*, 1874, Neue Pinakothek, Munich

The house in Argenteuil was close to the bank of the Seine, so Monet bought an old boat on which he could sketch and paint while floating downriver or anchored midstream. We see it in *The Studio Boat*, 1876 (Barnes Foundation, Philadelphia). Manet also pictured it in his *Claude Monet Painting in His Studio Boat*, 1874 (Neue Pinakothek, Munich, see above), with Monet seated at his easel and accompanied by his wife. While in Argenteuil Monet produced 259 paintings, 150 of them featuring scenes in and around the picturesque town.

Death of Camille

On 17 March 1878 Camille gave birth in Paris to her second son, Michel Monet (1878–1966). After the earlier birth a medical diagnosis suggested she had uterine cancer, and following this second one her health deteriorated. The Monets' domestic life was also complicated at the time. The art collector Ernest Hoschedé had gone bankrupt in 1877. He and his wife Alice (1844–1911) lost their Paris apartment and the house in Montgeron (both owned by Alice),

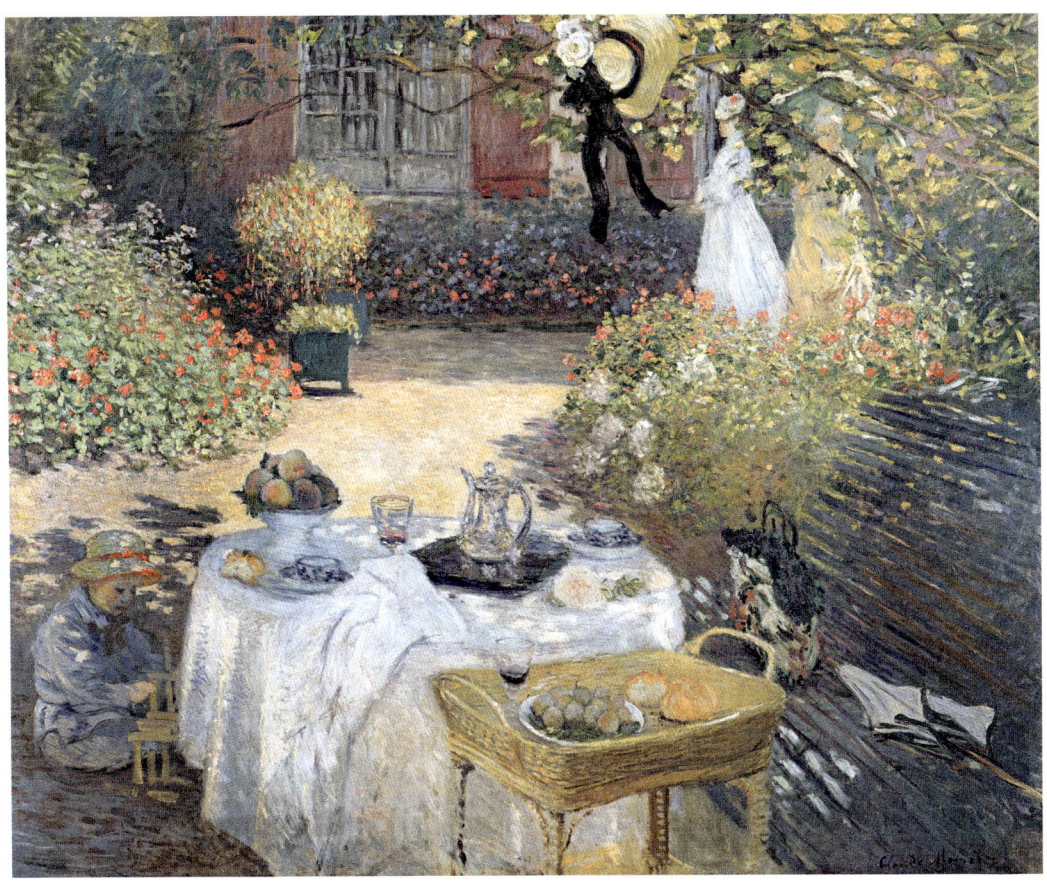

Claude Monet, *The Lunch*, ca. 1873, Musée d'Orsay, Paris

which were sold to pay his debtors. In July 1878 the Monets agreed to take in Alice and the children at the rented house in Vétheuil, northwest of Paris, while Hoschedé remained in Paris settling his affairs. Thirteen months later, on 5 September 1879, Camille Monet died after suffering a gruesome, prolonged illness. A distraught Monet rapidly sketched the deathbed scene then painted *Camille Monet on Her Deathbed* (Musée d'Orsay, Paris). Alice was also present and wrote of Camille's last moments, but Monet turned to paint; it was how he expressed

himself. Three weeks later he did write to his friend Pissarro: "I am devastated, not knowing where to turn or how I'll be able to organise my life with my two children. I am much to be pitied."

Alice Hoschedé

Alice Hoschedé (see pages 28/29) is thought to have begun an affair with Monet after he had visited the Hoschedé château in Montgeron in 1877.

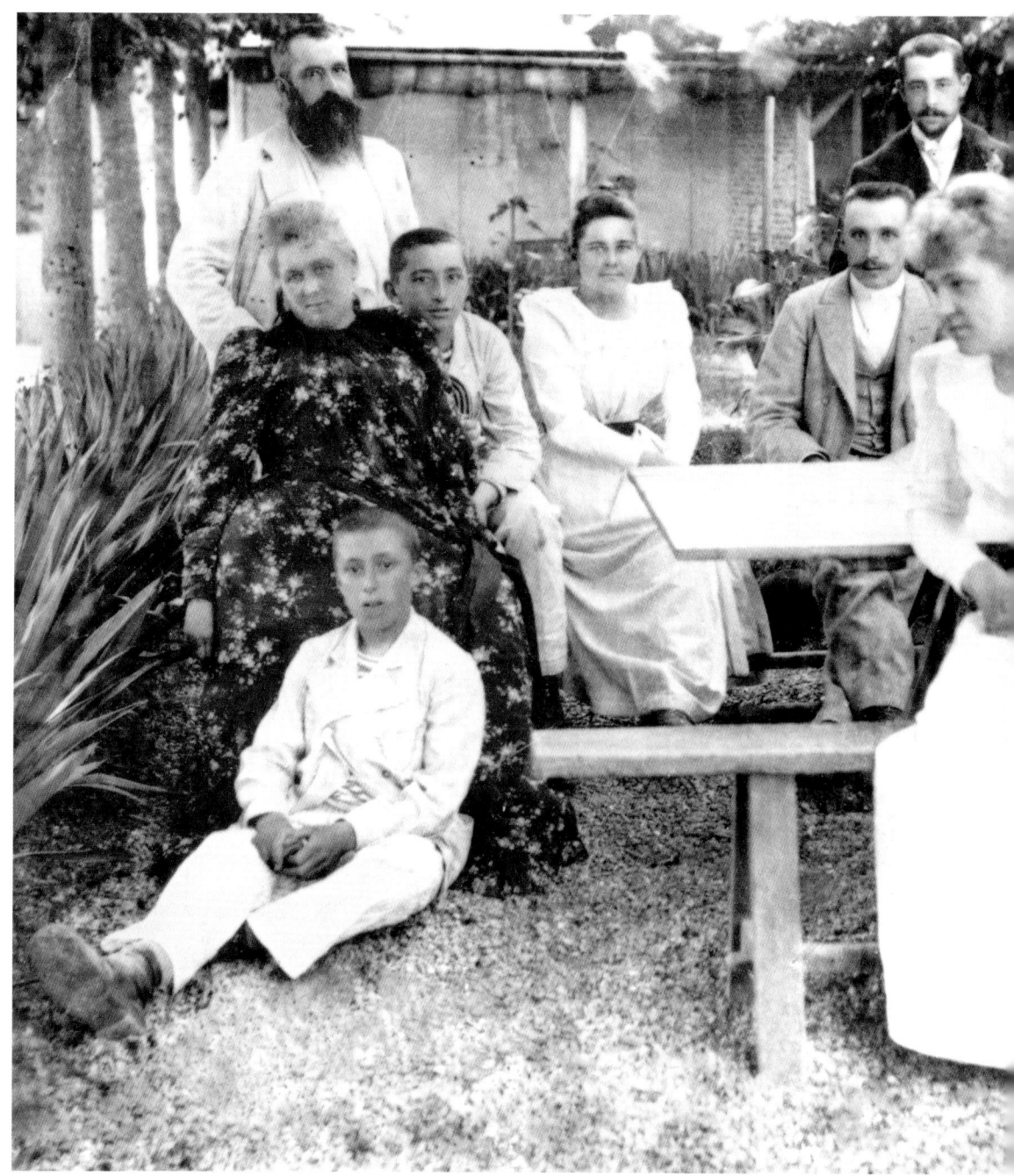

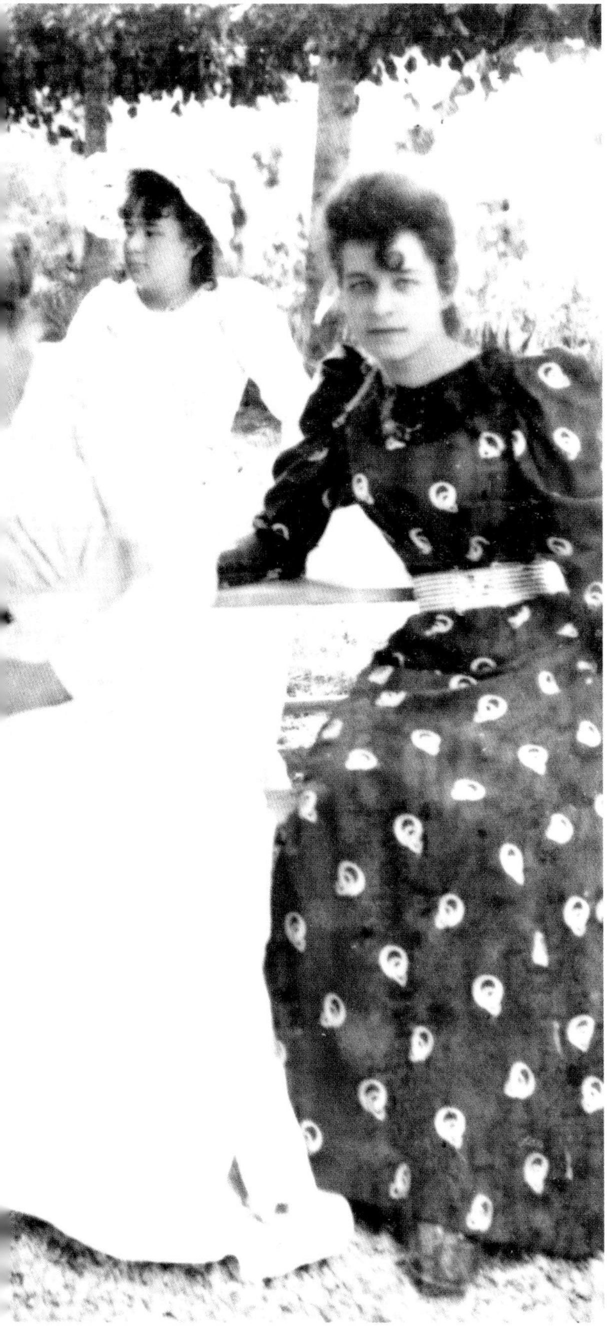

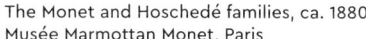

The Monet and Hoschedé families, ca. 1880,
Musée Marmottan Monet, Paris

Following the death of Camille, Alice looked after all the children, playing a kind of housekeeper/live-in mistress role. The Hoschedé children, with the exception of their daughter Marthe, called the artist "papa Monet". The pair made their relationship public in 1881 when they moved to Poissy with their joint family of eight children, organising local schools for them. Here Monet continued to work, producing art to sell.

He disliked Poissy but painted beautiful river scenes like *The Two Anglers*, 1882 (Private Collection). A superb black crayon drawing of this work survives (Fogg Museum, Harvard Art Museums, Cambridge, Mass.). It was created to illustrate an article in *L'Art Moderne* in 1883. To adjust to his new domestic life Monet immersed himself in work. He travelled to different places, including Dieppe and Varengeville-sur-Mer, always sketching and painting, finding a new angle, a different view. His interest in the Impressionists' annual shows had diminished, and he did not participate in those of 1880 and 1881. Following the death of Alice's estranged husband Ernest in 1891 Monet and Alice married on 16 July 1892. His friends the artist Gustave Courbet and Paul César Helleu witnessed the ceremony.

Marketing the "Impressionists"

Monet reconnected with Paul Durand-Ruel in October 1880 and many works were sold, which greatly improved his financial position. Durand-Ruel sent

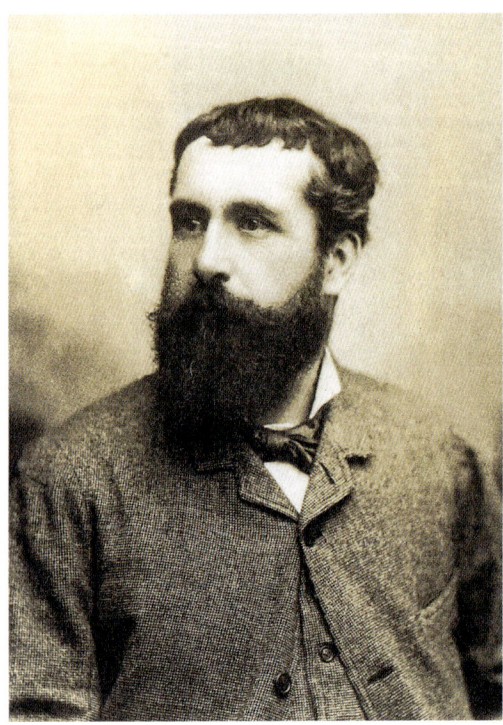

William Benque, *Claude Monet*, 1883, private collection

collections of Impressionist paintings to many exhibitions and gallery shows in France and elsewhere in Europe as well as to his own gallery in New York, which gave artists sales and publicity. Meanwhile, in 1882 Monet exhibited his work again at the seventh Impressionist exhibition alongside Gustave Caillebotte, Paul Gauguin, Armand Guillaumin. Berthe Morisot, Pissarro, Renoir and Alfred Sisley – a strong showing by the original Impressionist group. Monet exhibited thirty-five works dating from 1879 to 1882, mainly landscapes from in and around Vétheuil, including snow scenes and an architectural composition, *The Church at Vétheuil*, 1881 (Private Collection, see page 31). The following year Durand-Ruel organised five important one-man shows for Monet, Boudin, Renoir, Sisley and Pissarro. Monet's took place in March 1883. Records of monies paid to Monet by Durand-Ruel show that his paintings were selling. He was becoming prosperous, but it was still a period of uncertainty.

Giverny

In 1883 Monet left Paris to settle permanently in Giverny, around 50 miles northwest of the city, on the right bank of the Seine. The small farming community of around 300 inhabitants was located where the Seine is joined by its tributary the Epte. Monet rented a large, detached house, the Maison du Pressoir – an apple press was nearby – that was suitable for himself and Alice and their eight children, and a barn to use as a studio. The garden had potential; Monet was a keen gardener. The farmer owner, unaware of Monet's predilection for leaving properties without paying rent, was pleased to rent it to him. Monet's finances were still precarious, for selling paintings took time. He would live in this house for forty-three years (1883–1926) until his death, creating both an idyllic flower garden and a second one inspired by Japanese water gardens.

Just as he was moving in he received news of the death of Édouard Manet on 30 April. Manet's brother, the painter Eugène Manet, sent a telegram asking him to be a pall-bearer at the funeral. Monet had to borrow money from Durand-Ruel for the train fare and the cost of a mourning suit. Arts writers now speculated about who was the new leader of modern art in France, and their choice fell on Monet.

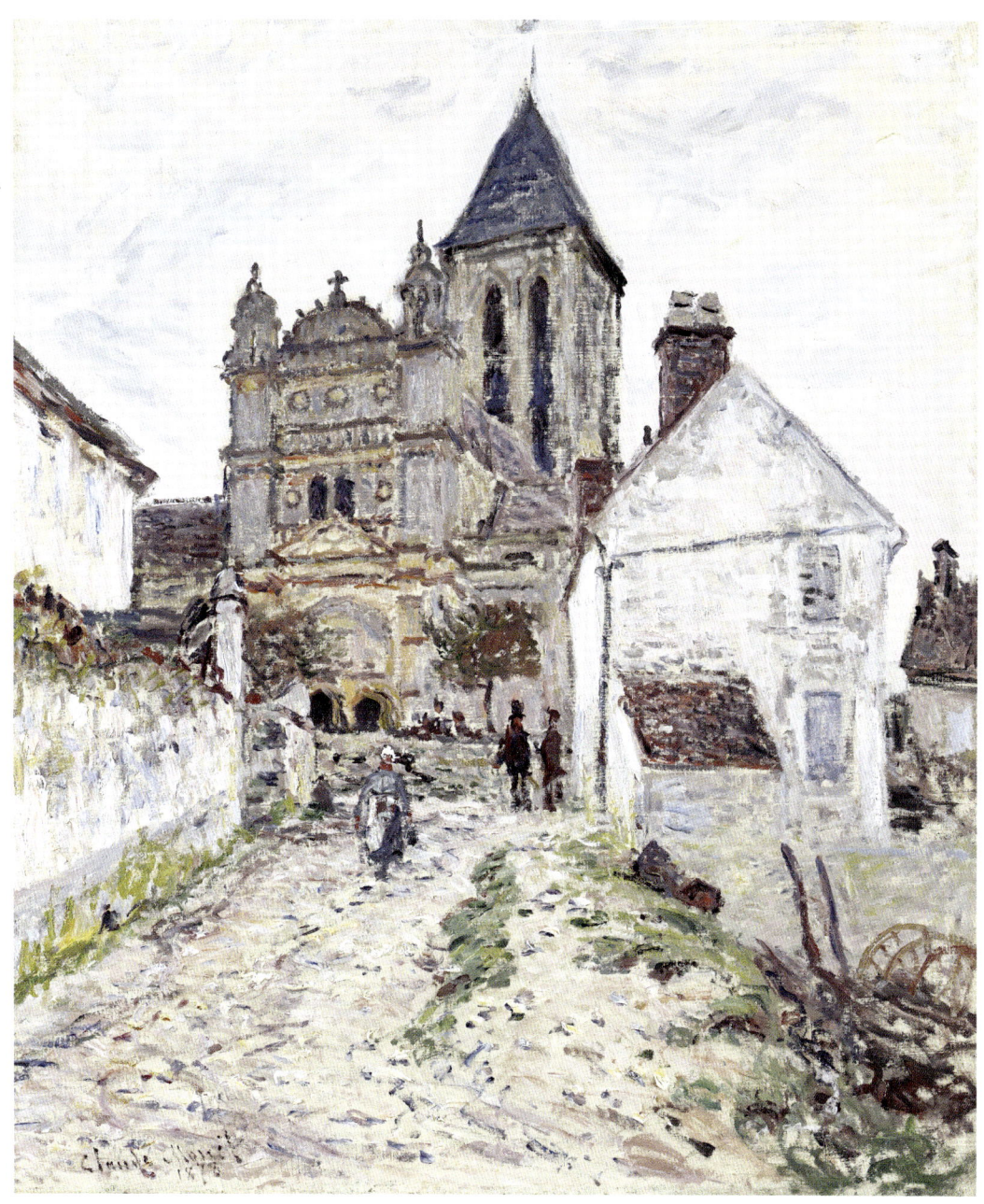

Claude Monet, *The Church at Vétheuil*, 1878, National Galleries of Scotland, Edinburgh

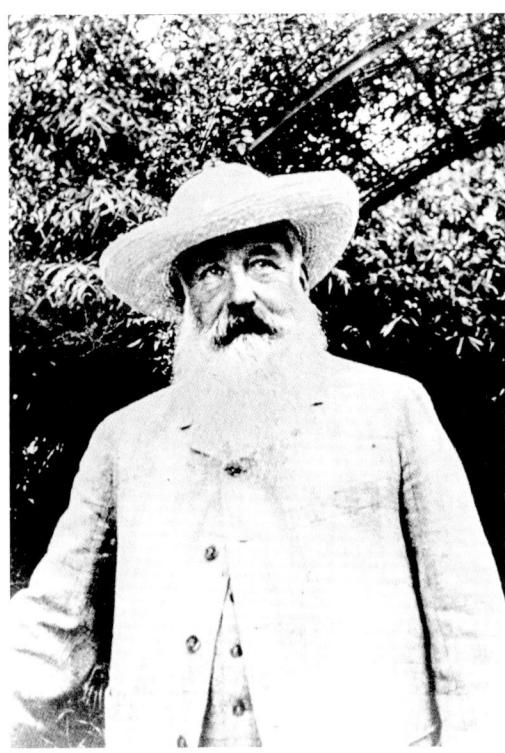

Sacha Guitry, *Portrait of Claude Monet at Giverny*, 1915,
Musée Marmottan Monet, Paris

Monet and Manet's *Olympia*

In 1889 Monet began a fund-raising campaign for the purchase of Manet's painting *Olympia*, which he hoped to see placed in a national collection. His efforts succeeded, as politicians and other artists pledged support. In November 1890 French newspapers announced that the painting had been acquired for the Musée du Luxembourg. Some still remembered the scandal the work had caused when

exhibited at the 1865 Salon. Its placement in a national museum was a breakthrough for contemporary French art, and it was all thanks to Monet.

"I want to paint the air"

A series of waterscapes painted by Monet in 1896/97 at Étretat on the Normandy coast concentrated on the reflections of the sky and trees at different times of day. Monet said that while artists may paint a bridge or a house or trees or people, he wanted to paint the air, a virtual impossibility. Monet almost succeeded in his atmospheric works, painting several canvases at one time and altering each one as the light or the weather changed. Many exhibitions now included his work. Newly wealthy, in 1899, 1900 and 1901 Monet returned to London to paint, usually staying for about two months. On each occasion he chose to paint scenes along the river Thames and stayed at the luxurious Savoy Hotel on the Strand, occupying two suites with balconies overlooking the river, one to paint in. He started almost 100 paintings, which he then finished in his studio in Giverny.

Other trips outside the country in search of motifs took him as far afield as Christiania (now Oslo). At home he made use of his favourite models, his step-daughters Blanche and Suzanne Hoschedé. Blanche (1865–1947) also became a painter and would marry her step-brother, Monet's older son Jean. Suzanne (1868–99) married the American Impressionist painter Theodore Earl Butler. The two appear together in Monet's painting *Blanche*

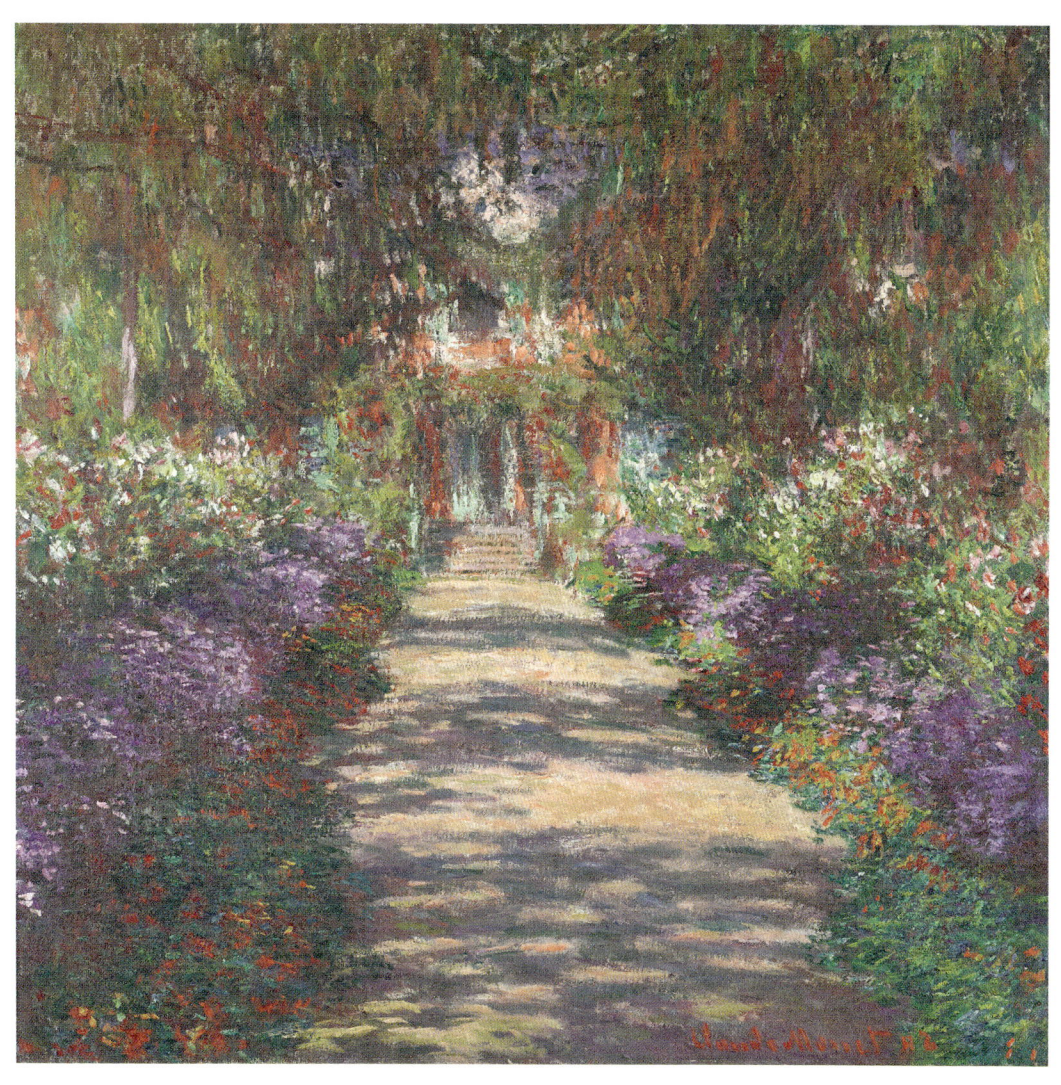

Claude Monet, *A Pathway in Monet's Garden, Giverny*, 1902, Österreichische Galerie Belvedere, Vienna

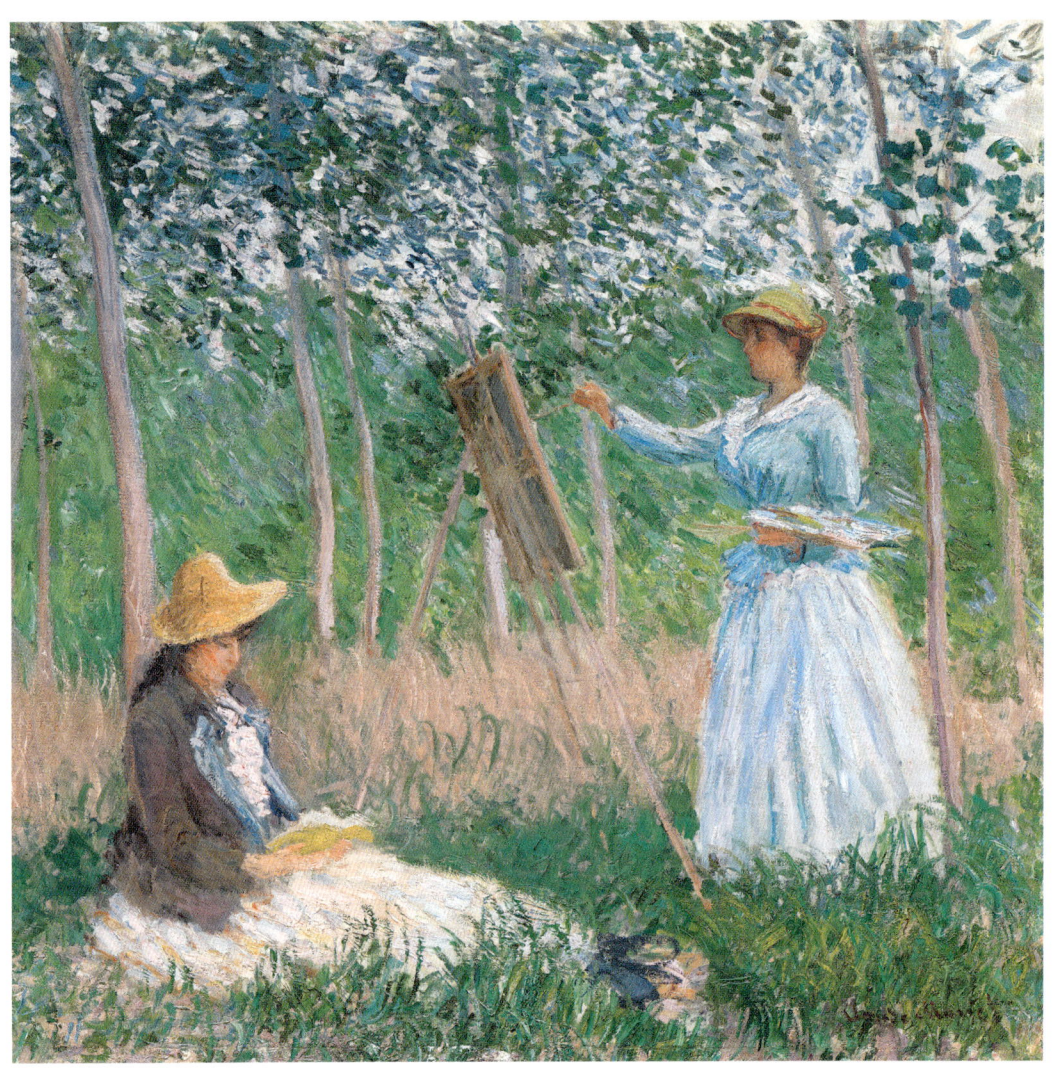

Claude Monet, *In the Woods at Giverny: Blanche Hoschedé at Her Easel with Suzanne Hoschedé Reading*, 1887, Los Angeles County Museum of Art, Mr. and Mrs. George Gard De Sylva Collection

Hoschedé at Her Easel with Suzanne Hoschedé Reading, 1887 (Los Angeles County Museum of Art, see page 34).

In October 1908 Monet and Alice visited Venice. There is a photograph of them feeding the pigeons in St Mark's Square (Musée Marmottan Monet, Paris). Monet was sorry he had never been there before, as it was an ideal location for an artist who loved to paint water and he determined to return. Back in Giverny Alice became unwell, and in the following months her health deteriorated. In 1910 she was diagnosed with spinal leukaemia. She died in May 1911. Monet was grief-stricken; he had lived with Alice for more than thirty years.

Painting Series

After painting a series of twelve views of the Gare St-Lazare in 1877 (page 75), Monet consciously developed a pattern of working on several canvases at once, capturing his motif at different times of day, perhaps in different months, focusing on the light, shadows and physical changes. In 1890 and 1891 he painted thirty canvases featuring the haystacks in a field near the house in Giverny (page 91) and in 1891 he concentrated on a row of tall poplar trees close to home (page 93). They were to be felled for wood, but Monet persuaded their owner to delay so he could paint them at different times during the summer and autumn. The resulting canvases, shown at Durand-Ruel's the following year, were commercial successes and he was now able to purchase the Giverny house.

In 1892/93 he ventured to Rouen on the river Seine in Normandy, around 40 miles north of Giverny, to paint aspects of a city famous for its cathedral (page 95). Monet focussed on the cathedral façade alone, capturing light and shadow on the building at different times of day. More than thirty canvases were the result, to be completed in Monet's Giverny studio during 1894.

First World War (1914–1918)

On the death of her husband Jean Monet in 1914 Blanche Hoschedé Monet moved into the Maison du Pressoir to keep house for her stepfather/father-in-law. As fellow painters they would enjoy their time together. When war broke out in Europe in 1914 the fighting was nearly at their doorstep; at times troops were only 30 miles away. At seventy-four Monet could do little but observe. After three years of "horribly cruel mourning" for Alice, Monet returned to painting. On 1 December 1914, he wrote: "Yesterday I resumed work … It's the best way to avoid thinking of these sad times. All the same, I feel ashamed to think about my little researches into form and colour while so many people are suffering and dying for us." His son Michel and stepson Jean-Pierre Hoschedé enlisted into the French army. Monet concentrated on his garden. From this period his series *Water Lilies with Weeping Willows* (1916–18) provides an expression of his contemplative mood. At the cessation of the war in Europe Monet offered a series of water-lily paintings as a gift to the French nation: "It's not

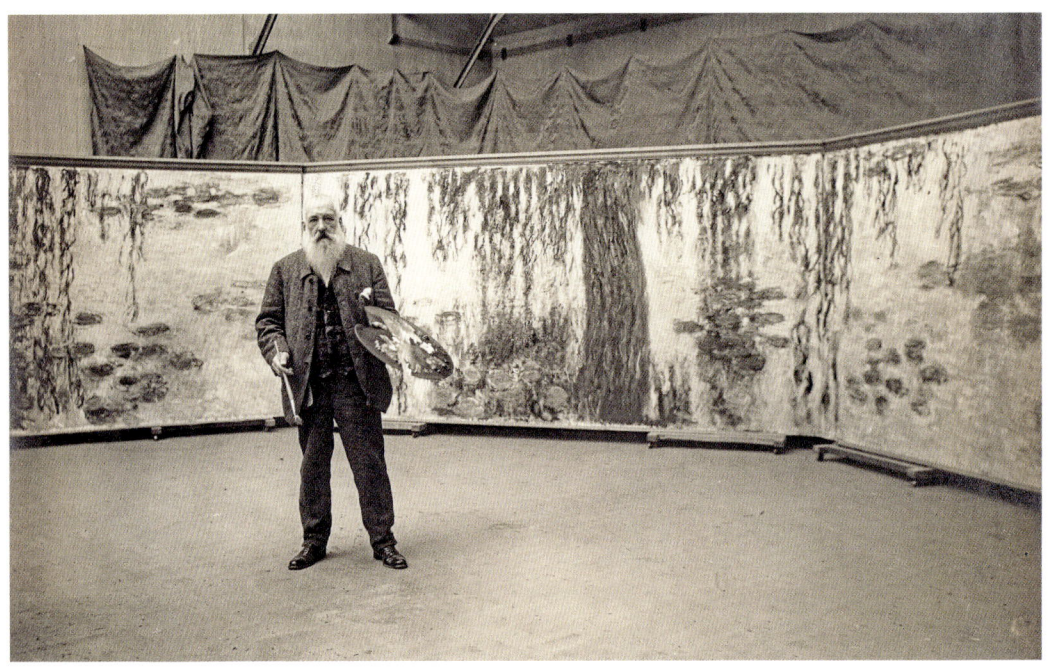

Henri Manuel, *Claude Monet with His Palette in Front of His Work 'Les Nymphéas'*, 1920s, private collection

much but it's the only way I have to take part in the victory," he wrote in a letter to the Prime Minister, his friend Georges Clemenceau (letter from Monet to Clemenceau, 12 November 1918).

After military service Michel Monet returned to live in a wing of the house at Giverny. A quiet man, he too painted. His love was for expensive cars and the model Gabrielle Bonaventure, an unmarried mother whom Monet would not allow in the house. They married after Monet's death.

Water Lilies at Giverny

As early as 1897 Monet began a series of paintings of water lilies at Giverny that continued until the end of his life. It started with his decision to buy a large plot of land across a road at the bottom of his gar-den. He set out to create a Japanese-inspired water garden, and with local council permission diverted river water from the Epte to create a large pond in which to plant exotic hybrid water lilies. Preliminary works had been seen by a journalist when he visited Monet's studio in 1898, writing about them in *La revue illustrée* (15 March, 1898). The inspiration was Monet's admiration for Japanese woodblock prints, particularly the work of Utagawa Hiroshige (1797–1858) and Katsushika Hokusai (1760–1849). The walls of Monet's home in Giverny were covered with his collection of them. Beginning in 1890 Monet had intensified his study of light on water, skies and buildings. It culminated in a remarkable cycle of paintings of water lilies shown in a landmark exhibition in 1909. In the remaining years of his life Monet concentrated on improving the water garden and painted innumerable views of it.

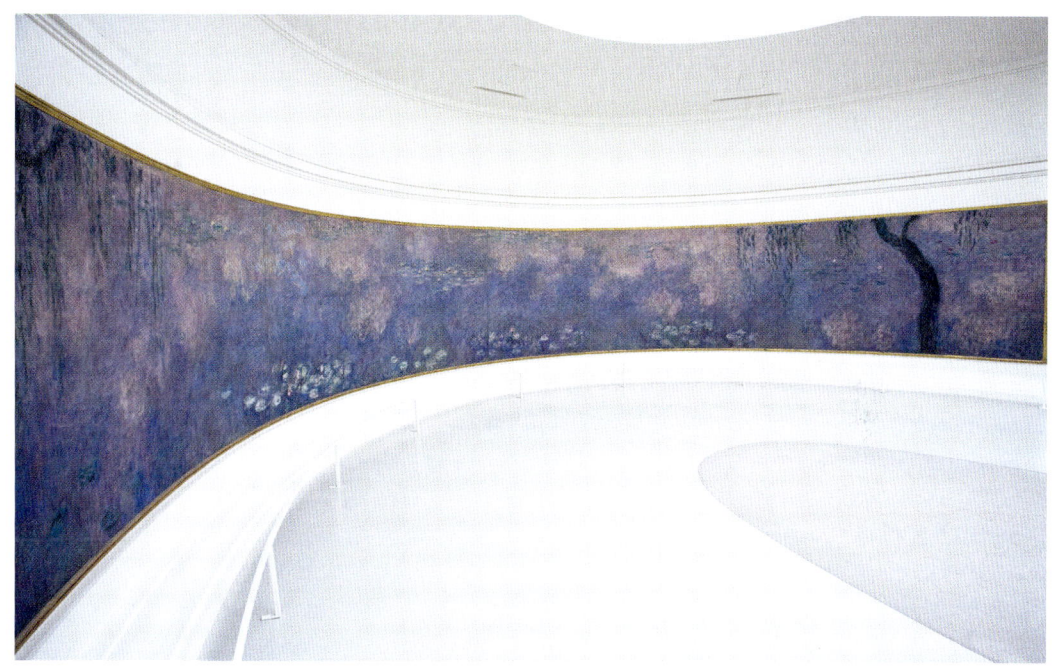

Exhibition of the *Nymphéas* series at the Musée de l'Orangerie, Paris

Late Paintings

In 1912 Monet experienced pain in his eyes and soon lost the sight in his right eye. He had developed cataracts. It affected his art in that his colour perception changed. He sought help – agreeing to three operations on his eye in 1923 – and wore prescription glasses made especially for him by Zeiss in 1924, which to some extent corrected his vision. He continued to paint, compensating for the deterioration of his eyesight. In later paintings of the garden pond Monet would eliminate its surroundings and focus on the water and the lilies and reflections of the sky and sun on the water.

Diagnosed with pulmonary sclerosis, after months of illness Oscar-Claude Monet died at Giverny on 5 December, 1926. He was eighty-six.

He was buried next to Alice in Giverny, and his funeral was attended by his family and by Clemenceau, Prime Minister of France. Monet's gift to France, the vast *Nymphéas (see page 36)*, had been completed just before his death. Twenty-two monumental canvases more than two metres in height and totalling ninety metres in length were placed in the Musée de l'Orangerie in Paris (see above) and displayed to the public in May 1927. Michel Monet inherited the Giverny estate. He died in a car accident in 1966.

Monet's house and gardens, the focus of his life for more than forty years, were bequeathed to the Musée Marmottan, overseen by the Musée des Beaux-Arts, Paris. Monet's private painting collection is in the museum. Today Monet's house and gardens, the distillation of the artist and his life, are open to the public.

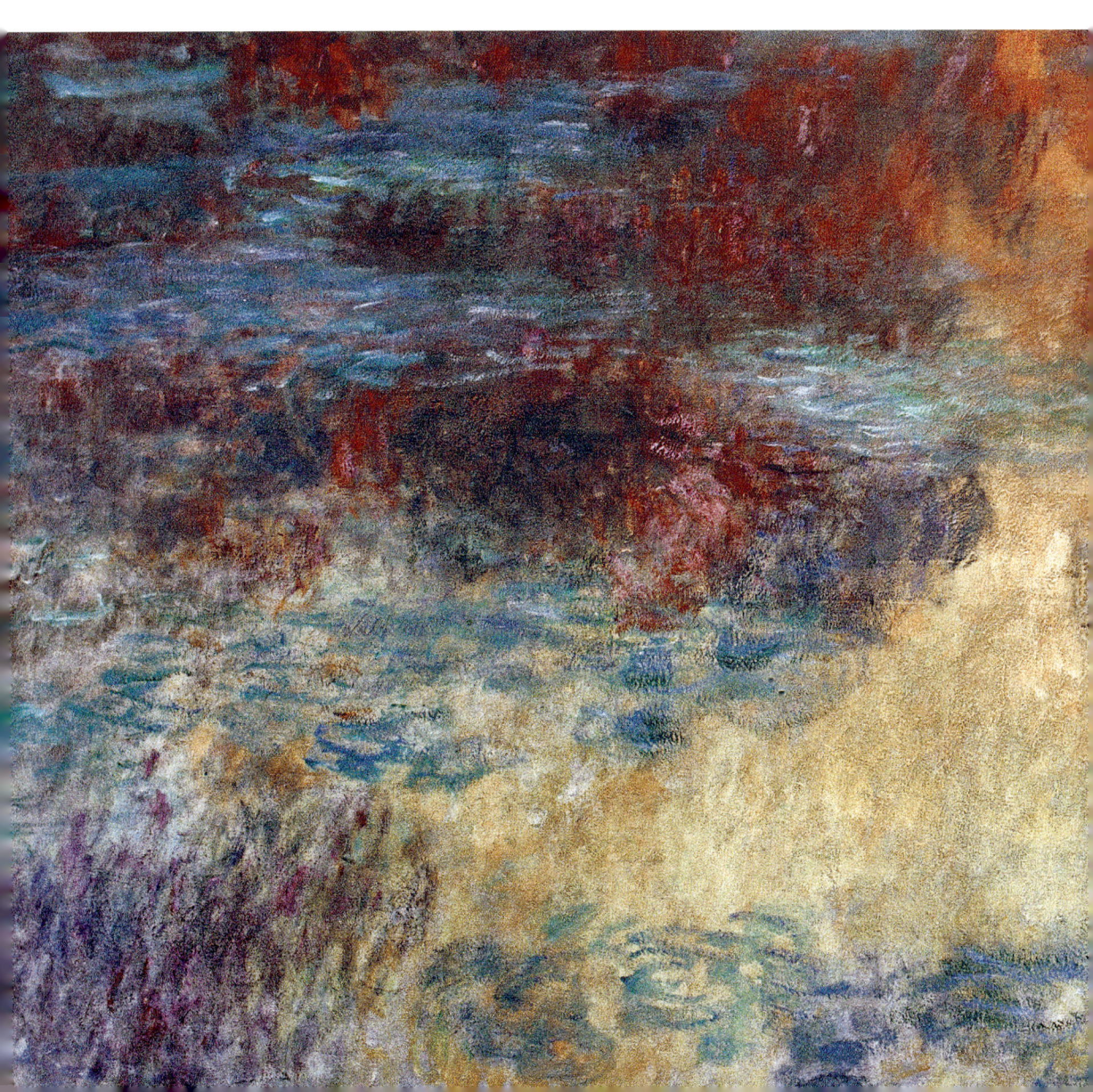

WORKS

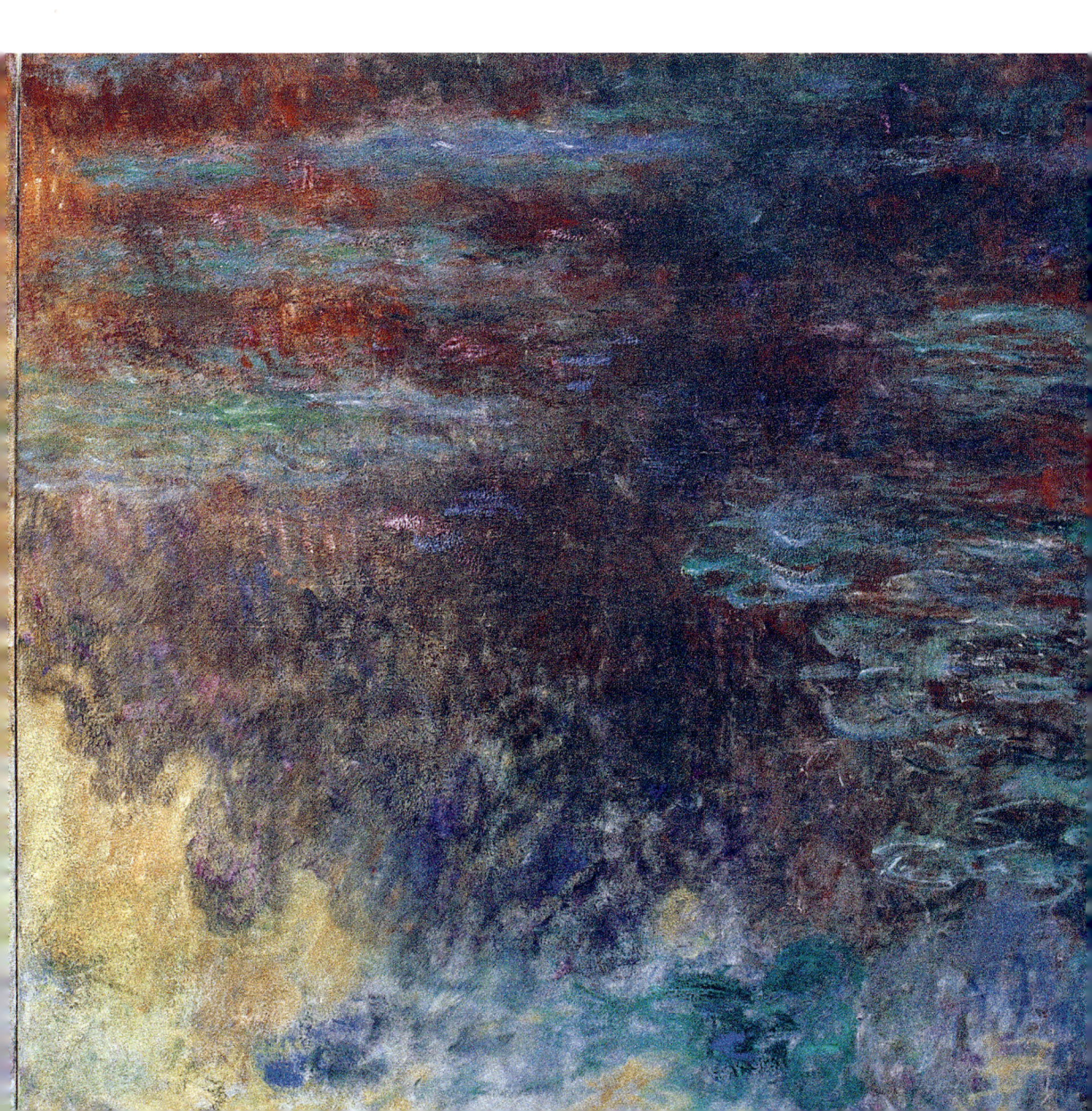

View at Rouelles, 1858

Oil on canvas
46 × 65 cm
Private Collection

One of the sites visited by Eugène Boudin and Claude Monet in 1858 was the village of Rouelles, on the northern outskirts of Le Havre, around 8 miles from its centre. There each of them chose a typical view of the lush, tranquil landscape. Boudin painted two canvases depicting the Rouelles valley landscape. Monet produced only one, the beautiful *View at Rouelles*. The work highlights Monet's skill as a painter not yet eighteen years old, one who was benefitting from Boudin's mentorship. The peaceful setting – the only movement being in the water and the clouds – did not require him to try to capture a momentary impression of what he saw.

It would be Monet's first publicly exhibited painting, shown at the *Exposition municipal de la ville du Havre* that same year. It was signed and dated "O. Monet 58". In this idyllic pastoral scene a winding stream appears in the foreground, with a lone fisherman seated on its bank lending scale to the composition. The man's blue smock and brimmed straw hat attest to the warm, sunny weather. The small stream curves through the pasture from the right before flowing toward the viewer with reflections of its bank and the tall trees in the distance. In the middle distance are various trees of different shapes and sizes and a sloping field of wheat can be glimpsed at right. In the background a distant hill stretches across the picture space. Closer to the viewer a row of stick-straight trees direct the eye upward toward the blue sky and drifting clouds. Monet's use of sunlight and shadow reflected in the water and on the green pasturage and trees is masterful. It is a remarkable work, which shows how much Monet had absorbed Boudin's style of painting en plein air. Monet kept the painting for many years before parting with it and two other canvases – *The Banks of the Seine at Le Petit-Gennevilliers,* 1874, and *The Old Rue de la Chausée at Argenteuil,* 1872 – in January 1877, when he presented them to François Fayette, headmaster of the École Préparatoire des Arts et Métiers in Argenteuil, possibly in payment of his son Jean's school fees incurred in 1876.

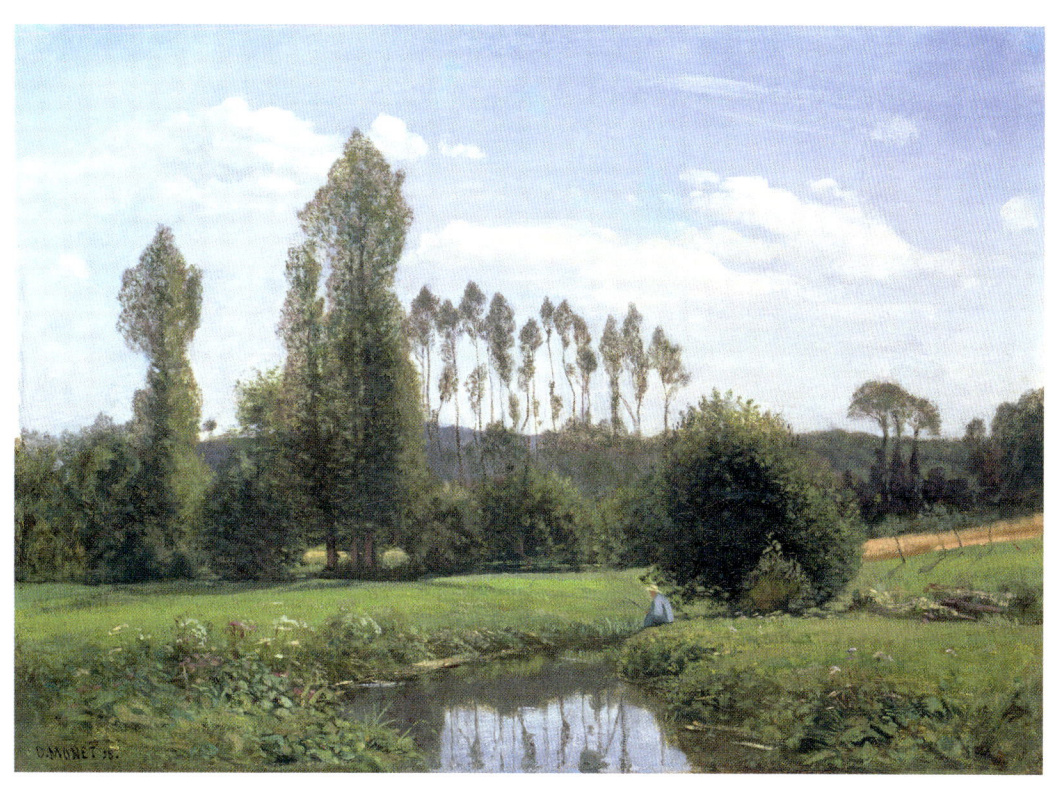

La Pointe de la Hève at Low Tide, 1865

Oil on canvas
90.2 × 150.5 cm
Kimbell Art Museum, Fort Worth

This seashore landscape was exhibited at the Paris Salon in 1865, one of the two marine paintings that were his first submissions to the prestigious event.

In that year the Salon hung its paintings alphabetically by the artist's surname. Monet's flanked Édouard Manet's *Olympia*, 1865 (Musée d'Orsay, Paris) which was to cause a furore. Moreover, some critics confused Monet's name with Manet's, which did not please either artist.

La Pointe de la Hève at Low Tide received favourable reviews from the Salon judges and art critics. To create the work, Monet first painted a smaller canvas that he could carry directly onto the shingle beach. It was a spot he had known well since childhood. That preparatory work, *La Pointe de la Hève, Sainte-Adresse*, 1864, is now in the National Gallery, London. Monet took that canvas back to his studio to copy on a larger scale. The point of view is that of a stroller along the shoreline. The dramatic sky and rough sea are replicated in quick dabs of paint using a flat brush in what would later be called an Impressionist style.

A horse-drawn cart is heading away from the viewer through the shallow surf and a pair of white horses are being led alongside. A man with a stick follows behind. The overall effect is highly dramatic, with cumulonimbus clouds threatening heavy rain but in the far distance a break in the clouds that allows sunlight to fall on a distant stretch of gravel beach. Whitecaps on the deep green waves indicate the strength of the wind. At the right two small boats have been drawn high up the shingle.

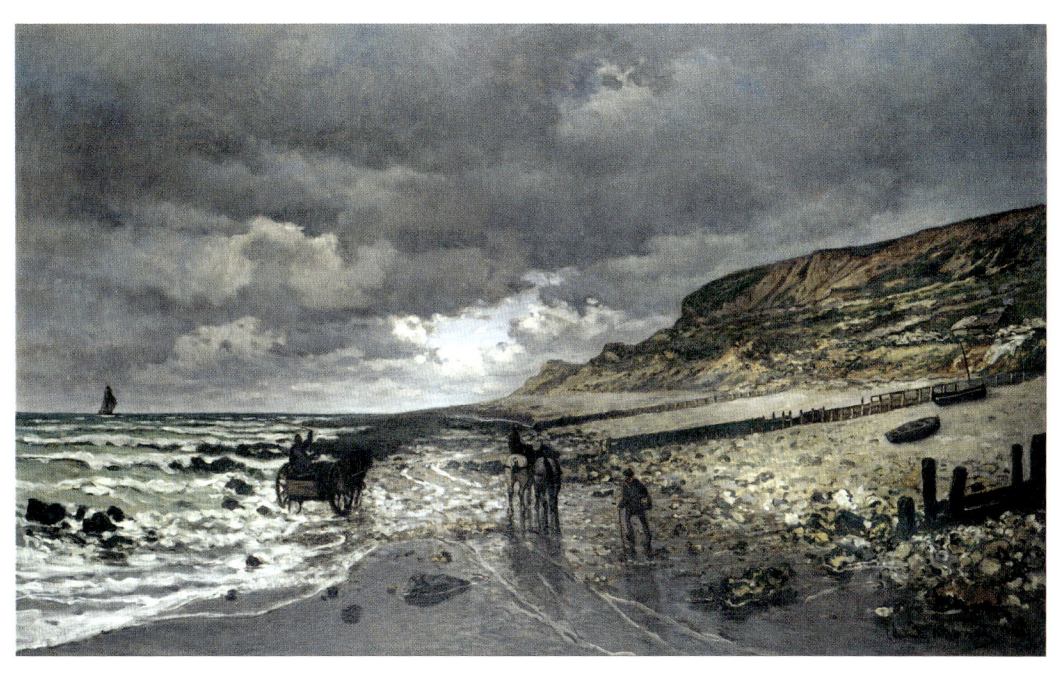

The Luncheon on the Grass, 1865/66

Oil on canvas
130 × 181 cm
Pushkin Museum, Moscow

Following Édouard Manet's controversial *The Luncheon on the Grass* from 1863 (Musée d'Orsay, Paris), Monet produced a non-provocative version. It was a popular subject for painters. In this preliminary version there are twelve figures representing a group of friends relaxing in a forest glade with a luncheon spread out on a tablecloth beneath the trees where dappled sunlight filters through onto the forest floor. The male figures include Monet's painter friend Frédéric Bazille in various poses and French painter Albert Lambron des Piltieres (b. 1836–after 1869), a fellow student of Charles Gleyre's. Monet planned to exhibit a much larger painting of this scene at the annual Paris Salon in 1866 but ran out of time to finish it. This is the preliminary painting, begun around September 1865, painted in his studio from preparatory life studies.

Monet's much larger painting of the same scene begun in October 1865 remained unfinished by mid March 1866, and was not submitted to the Paris Salon that year. Only two sections survive; part of it was lost owing to damage during storage. It was in Monet's possession until 1878 when he left it as a rental pledge, a security in lieu of money owed to the owner of the house Monet rented in Argenteuil. When he retrieved the vast canvas in 1884 he found part of it destroyed by mould. He cut out the damaged area, leaving two panels of different dimensions (Musée d'Orsay, Paris). Monet regularly returned to the setting of a pleasurable lunch outdoors. *The Luncheon*, ca. 1873 (Musée d'Orsay, Paris), painted in the garden of the house in Argenteuil, pictures a table with the remains of a finished meal and Monet's young son Jean, around five years old, seated nearby on the ground.

Precedents for such scenes were the *fêtes galantes* made popular by the French artist Jean-Antoine Watteau (1684–1721), including *Les Champs Elysees*, ca. 1720–21, and *The Halt during the Chase*, ca. 1717/18 (both Wallace Collection, London). Gustave Courbet's *The Huntsman's Picnic*, 1858 (Wallraf-Richartz-Museum, Cologne), and Édouard Manet's *Music in the Tuileries Gardens*, 1862 (The National Gallery, London), were more contemporary reworkings.

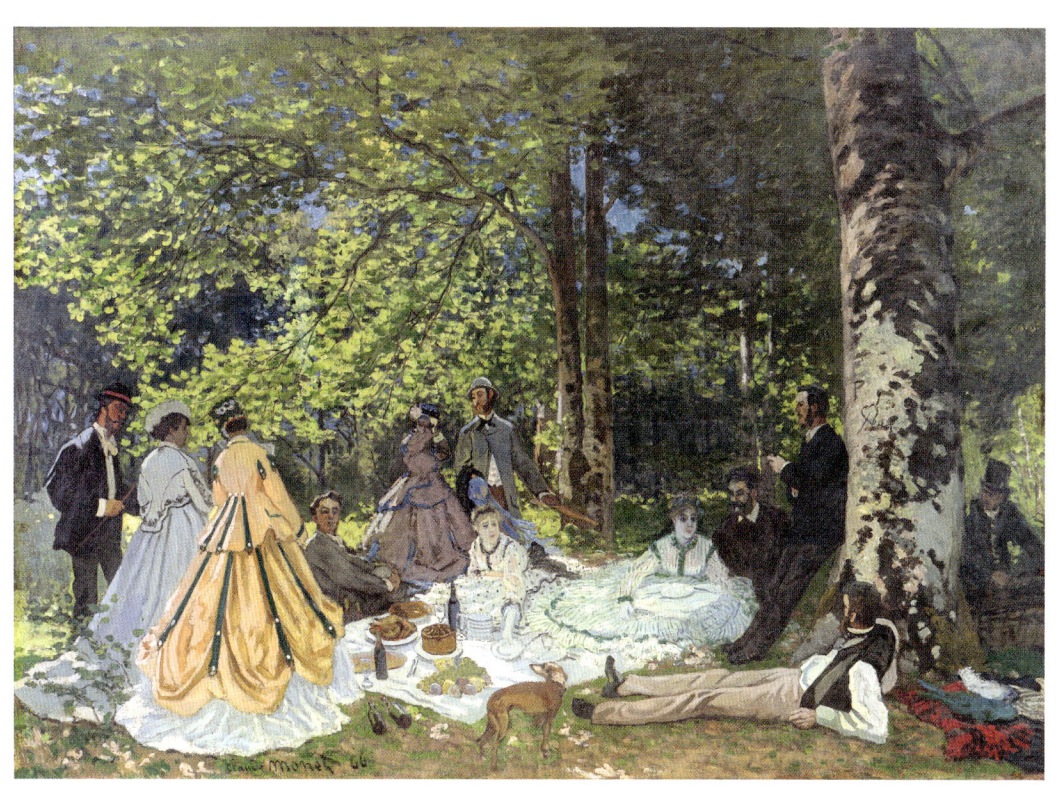

Women in the Garden, ca. 1866

Oil on canvas
255 × 205 cm
Musée d'Orsay, Paris

Women in the Garden was begun in the spring of 1866, painted in his garden at a rented house in Ville-d'Avray, a suburb west of Paris. He chose a vertical, portrait-style composition. The canvas was monumental in size, and in order to be able to reach the upper part of it Monet dug a trench into which it could be lowered by means of a pulley. The painting was then finished in his studio at Honfleur during the winter.
The life-size composition depicts four young women, two standing and chatting, one in motion, possibly picking flowers, and one seated on the ground beneath a tree and shading herself from the sun with a parasol. Monet wanted to capture the pleasure of a gathering of friends, the atmosphere of a moment in time, the beauty of the bright, clear day and the woodsy setting. Camille, the artist's companion, posed for the three figures on the left. He tricked the eye with the creation of dappled shade from the trees and foliage and shadow of branches across the seated woman's brilliantly white skirt. For the style of the dresses Monet looked at illustrations in fashion magazines; the same dresses appear in the incomplete *Luncheon on the Grass,* 1865/66. At this time Monet was in dire straits financially, and it would seem unlikely that the dresses were purchased, though Camille had her own wardrobe. Monet's mentor and friend the painter Eugène Boudin also had useful contacts. The dresses appear in Boudin's own drawings from the 1860's as well.
There is a distinct realism in Monet's portrayal, as if the viewer were only feet away from the group. But the painting was rejected by the Salon of 1867 for want of a strong narrative. One jury member drew attention to the thick brushstrokes, clearly visible, suggesting that it was laziness on the part of the artist to paint in this way. The writer and art critic Émile Zola (1840–1902) felt that the painting captured *la vie moderne.* He commented on the strong light and shadow: "The sun fell straight on to dazzling white skirts; the warm shadow of a tree cut out a large grey piece from the paths and the sunlit dresses. The strangest effect imaginable. One needs to be singularly in love with his time to dare to do such a thing, fabrics sliced in half by the shadow and the sun." What is evident is Monet's close attention to detail, such as the tiny glimpse of a crinoline under the dress of the woman seated on the ground. The painting was purchased from Monet by Frédéric Bazille in May 1867.

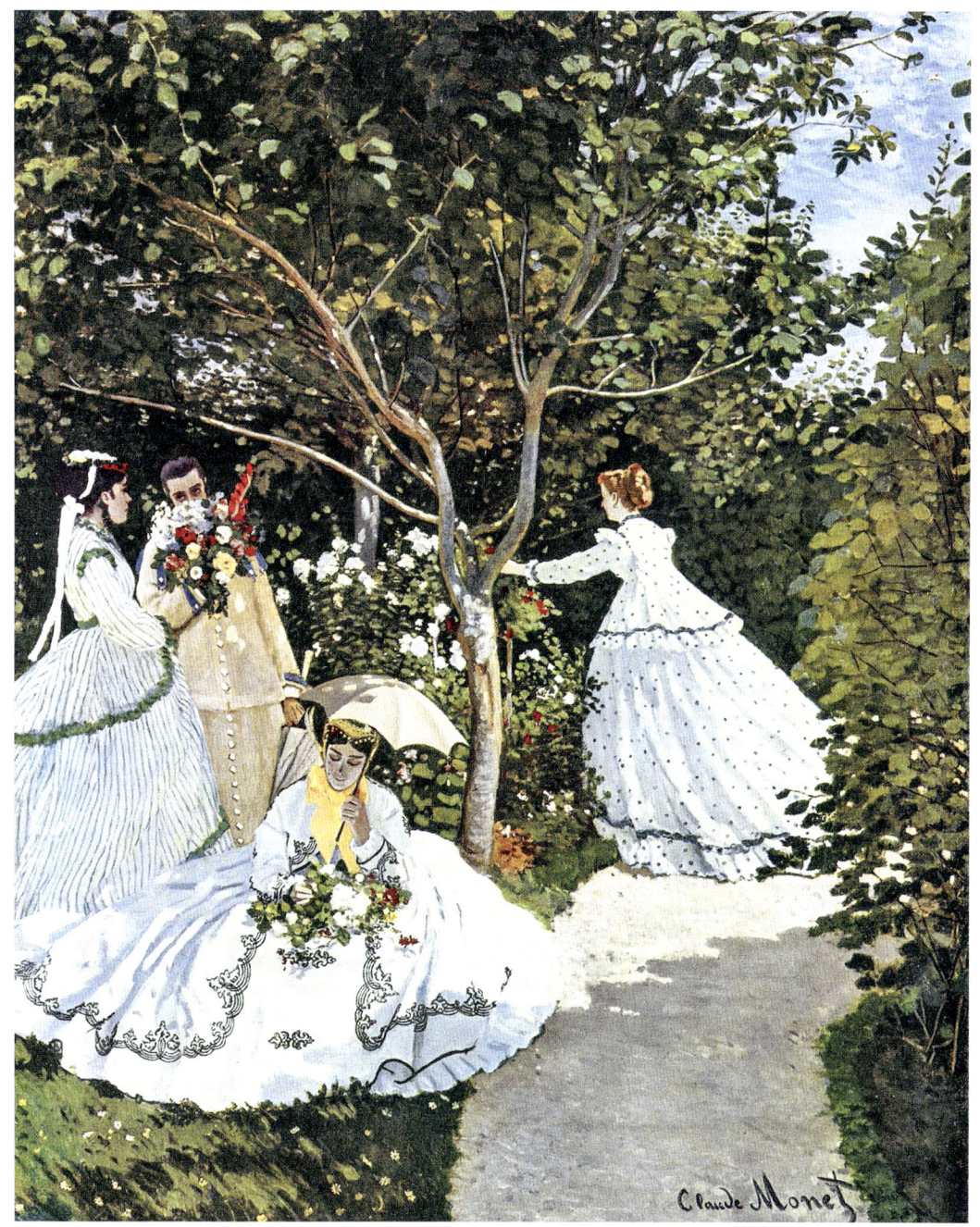

Camille, or The Woman in the Green Dress, 1866

Oil on canvas
231 × 151 cm
Kunsthalle Bremen

When exhibited as *Camille* at the 1866 Paris Salon this painting won Monet a silver medal. It is a full-length portrait of his nineteen-year-old girlfriend and model elegantly clothed, wearing a green-and-black-striped silk dress, a fur-trimmed velvet jacket, and a matching "Empire"-style bonnet. Camille was known for her fashion sense and in this work she carries the whole painting with the stunning sweep of her *robe de promenade or outdoor walking dress* popular with stylish women. Camille's momentary look to the side provides a glimpse of her face as she adjusts a hat ribbon. It appears as if she is moving away from the viewer.

Monet Initially included a patterned carpet, but painted over it leaving the floor plain and a deep-red curtain as backdrop to concentrate attention on the dress. The work was a landmark in Monet's professional career, bringing him his first recognition by the Salon and attention from art critics. The large-scale painting received very favourable reviews. Previously unfamiliar with the artist's work, Émile Zola (1840–1902) praised him for the "freshness of [his] painting style". He specifically referred to the dress and to Camille: "… It trails softly, it is alive, it declared loud and clear who this woman is." Another art critic, Théophile Thoré-Bürger (1807–69), commented on Camille: "… trailing a magnificent green silk dress, as dazzling as the fabrics painted by Veronese".

The absence of a steel-ribbed crinoline undergarment gave the dress a timeless look. Other critics were a little confused; was it by Manet or Monet? There was a similarity in the painting's bold use of black, a signature of Manet's art. The painting also received the attention of *La Vie Parisienne* with a caricature drawing of Camille and that dress titled "The Portrait of This Year's Salon", published on 5 May 1866.

Camille's costume, almost the exact same dress paired with a fur-trimmed jacket, had been illustrated in the *Petit Courier des Dames* from 18 November 1865. Did Monet or Camille buy the dress? Monet's friend Frédéric Bazille mentioned renting a green silk dress in a letter to his mother in January 1866.

Two years later the painting won Monet another accolade, a silver medal at the *Exposition Maritime du Havre*. At this exhibition *Camille* was sold to the director of the *Revue du XIXe siècle*, Arsène Houssaye (1814–96), a publisher, poet and writer on fashion well known in Parisian art circles. He paid 800 francs for it. Monet also received a commission to paint a smaller version from an American buyer.

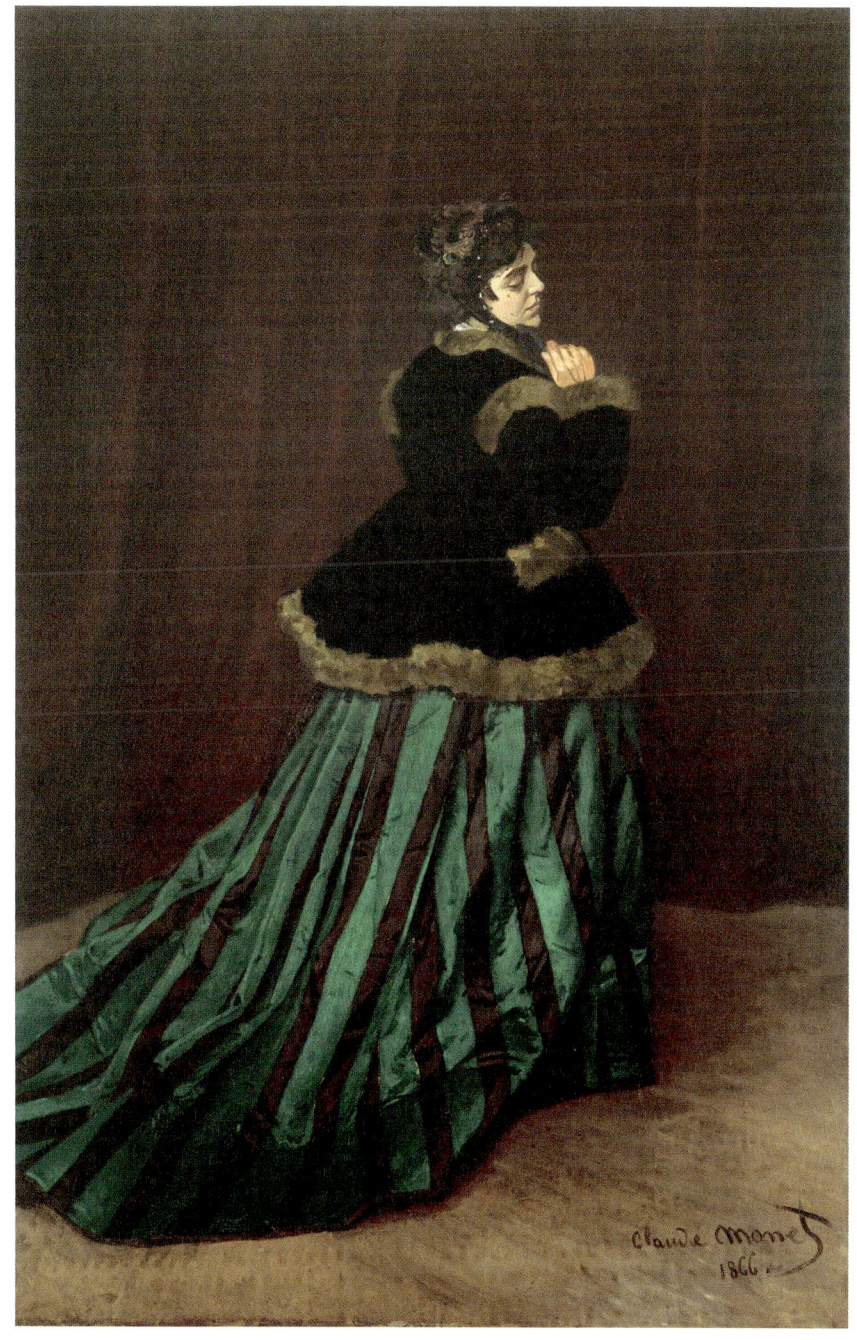

Garden at Sainte-Adresse, 1867

Oil on canvas
98.1 × 129.9 cm
The Metropolitan Museum of Art, New York

Monet painted this canvas while visiting his family in Le Havre in June 1867. He was twenty-six, and his girlfriend and model Camille was expecting their baby in August. Monet had enjoyed a successful showing at the annual Paris Salon but needed money and went home to produce several paintings that included members of his family and their properties in Sainte-Adresse.

In its composition, narrative, colouring and painting style the work is one of Monet's early masterpieces. It features his father wearing a Panama hat and seated in the foreground on the sea-view terrace of the Lecadre home. The two women with parasols are his cousins, and the man standing at the railing is his uncle. Monet focused on the sunlit garden, the sea view, and the figures at leisure. He paid close attention to details, from the yachts in the distance and ships with smoke billowing from their funnels beyond to the fashionable attire of his family members posing on the terrace.

Monet divided the canvas into three horizontal bands. The bottom section focuses on the architectural space of the garden terrace, its beds of gladioli, nasturtiums and geraniums, its comfortable seating and the four figures. The middle section presents the sea in a rich blue-green and with waves driven by the stiff breeze indicated by the fluttering flags. Stretching above the horizon is a pale blue, sunlit sky with clouds in the distance. The couple conversing at the edge of the terrace and a sailboat just beyond them tie the seascape together with the foreground scene.

Monet's composition accentuates the flatness of the depiction, informed by Japanese art as seen in the woodblock prints then circulating in Europe. Yet his painting style was adaptable. In this same period he painted the strikingly different *Street in Sainte-Adresse*, 1867 (Clark Art Institute, Williamstown, Mass.), which depicts a dirt road leading into the small town. Twelve years later, in April–May 1879, Monet exhibited *Garden at Sainte-Adresse* at the fourth Impressionist exhibition in Paris. Edgar Degas insisted that the exhibition be called an "Exposition des artistes indépendants", to emphasise that it was not a tight group of painters but a collection of individual artists. Some of the painters from the group's first show were missing, but it included for the first time Mary Cassatt and Paul Gauguin. The exhibition was a success; the artists shared its 16,000 visitors' entrance fees. Monet showed some twenty paintings, but *Garden at Sainte-Adresse* failed to sell.

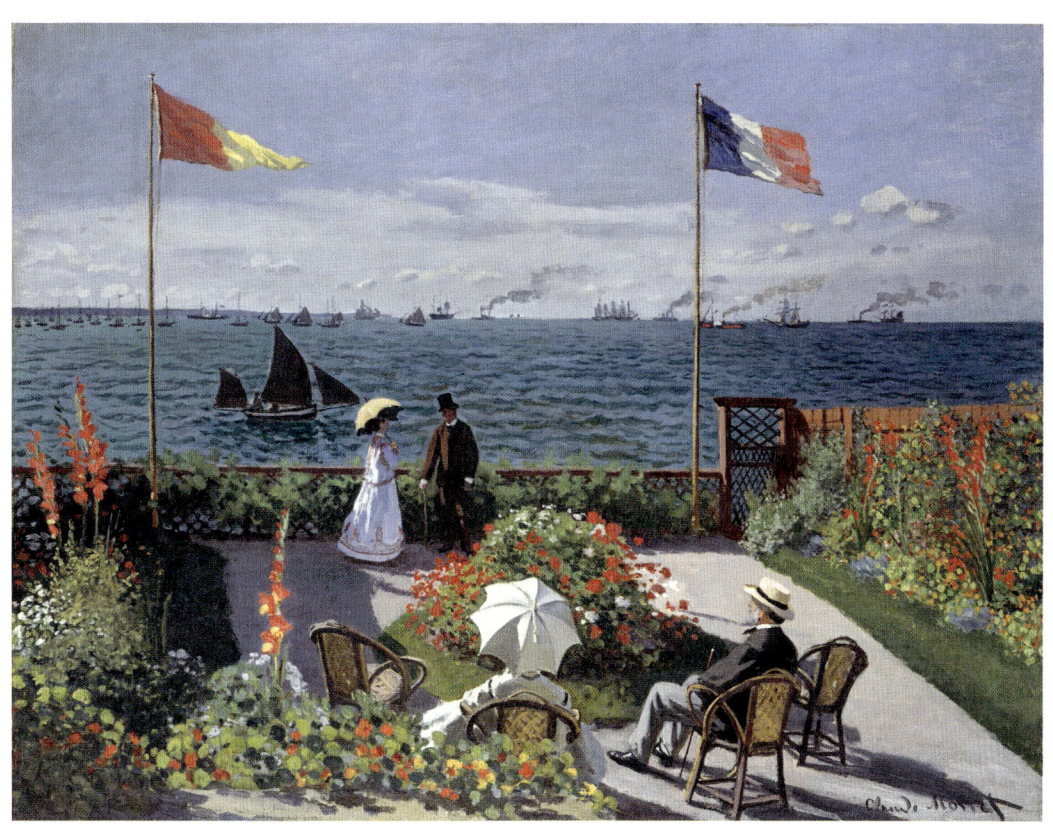

Madame Louis-Joachim Gaudibert, 1868

Oil on canvas
216.5 × 138.5 cm
Musée d'Orsay, Paris

Louis-Joachim Gaudibert (died 1870) was a well-known man in Le Havre society, a wealthy shipping insurer. As he was a friend and patron of Monet's, his parents commissioned the artist to paint Louis-Joachim's portrait. It was not to the liking of the parents, who refused it. Monet was greatly in need of money and in September 1868 Gaudibert gave him another chance, commissioning two portraits from him, one of his wife Marguerite and one of their young son, the three-year-old Louis-Eugène. The composition of the present one shows Monet re-creating aspects of his painting *Camille* from two years before. The curtain backdrop, the style of the dress and the figure's movement are similar. Madame Gaudibert, born Marguerite Marcel (1840–77), is painted full-length in three-quarter profile, slightly turning her head away from the viewer. The vertical composition accentuates her figure and the sumptuous dress. Her stance and her face in profile give the impression of a moment captured, like a photograph. Monet portrayed Madame Gaudibert putting on her gloves with her hat placed on a small table behind her, suggesting that she is preparing to go out. The richly patterned cashmere shawl, a status symbol of wealth usually worn by married or engaged women, is wrapped low around her waist in another indication of her fashion sense. The floor-length silk dress the colour of burnished copper dominates the picture. Monet captured the light and shadow in its folds while depicting it as a fashionable dress with a half-crinoline and an extended train. The style of the dress and her pose suggest that Monet had studied the latest illustrations in fashion magazines. The colours of the dress and shawl are repeated in the floral carpet and the roses in a vase on the table. The setting was the Château des Ardennes-Saint-Louis on the outskirts of Le Havre.

The portrait of young Louis-Eugène Gaudibert was a success. Monet captured the young boy with his head of blond curls and smiling with a book open on his lap. Marguerite Gaudibert's family was also known to Monet. Her father, a lawyer and notary in Le Havre, had been the subject of one of Monet's caricatures created more than ten years before – *Eugène Marcel*, 1855/56 (The Art Institute of Chicago). In 1868 bailiffs were confiscating paintings as payment for Monet's outstanding debts. To avoid this, Monet sent some to his aunt Marie-Jeanne Lecadre in Le Havre for safekeeping. His father's allowance had been withdrawn on the news of Monet's illegitimate baby. Louis-Joachim Gaudibert's commissions temporarily saved him; pleased with the portraits, Gaudibert arranged to help Monet with a regular allowance.

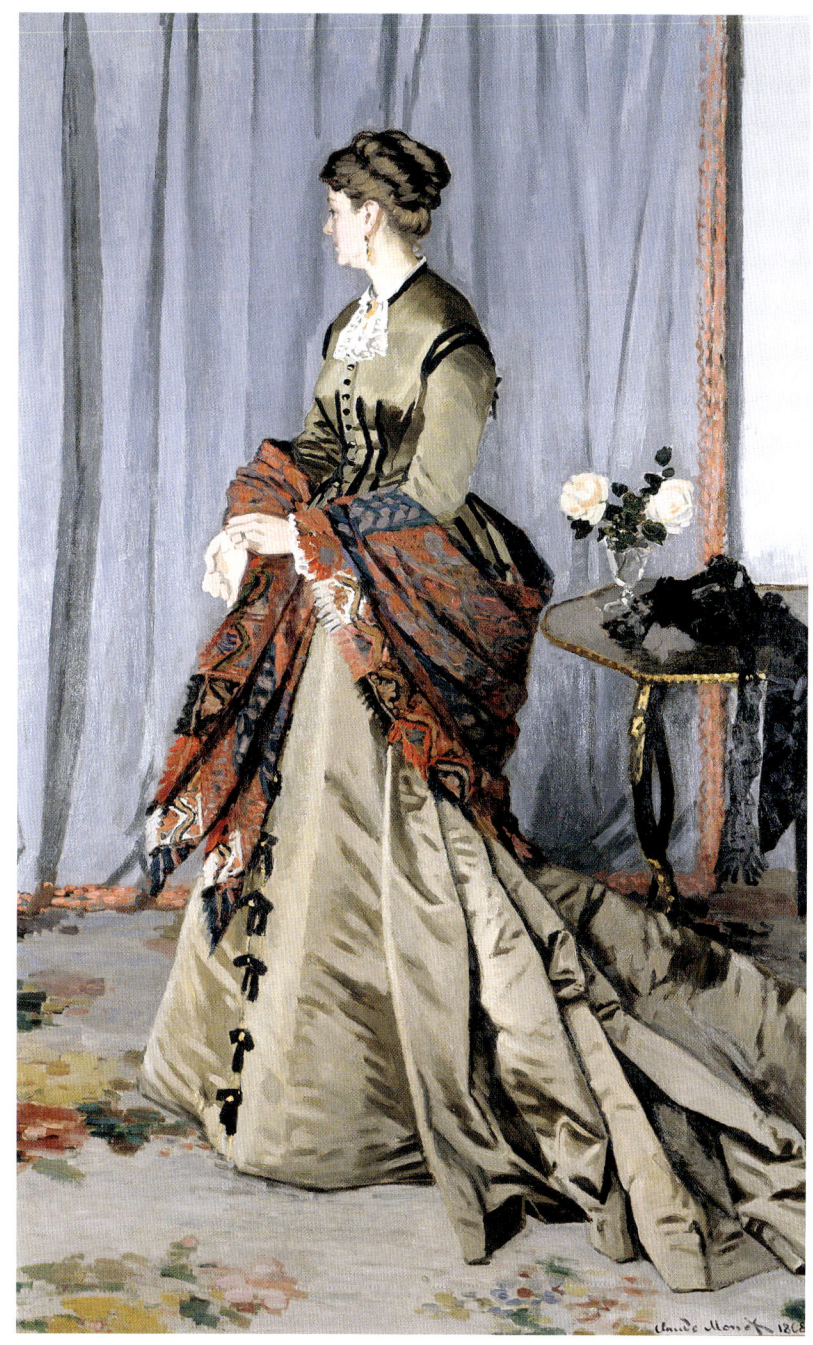

The Luncheon, 1868

Oil on canvas
231.5 × 151.5 cm
Städel Museum, Frankfurt am Main

From the moment of his birth Monet and Camille's first son was included in many paintings. This large artwork depicts a mother and son at a dining table. Jean is seated in a high chair, napkin tucked under his chin and with silver spoon in hand. On the table are boiled eggs, a bottle of wine, preserves and fruit and a loaf of bread. The child's mother, seated next to the boy, has laid her arm around his shoulders. In the background a maidservant has opened a cupboard door. Is it a hotel dining room, a restaurant, or a domestic setting? Monet does not reveal the location. In the foreground another place has been set, a plate with two boiled eggs, a chunk of bread, cutlery and a napkin. The chair has been pulled back, possibly by an unseen person who has momentarily stepped away, perhaps the painter. This glimpse into everyday life was started in the winter of 1868/69 when Monet and Camille were living in Étretat. The table and chairs are similar to those in two other interior compositions painted at this time: *The Dinner*, 1868/69 (Collection Emil Bührle, Zürich), featuring Jean and Camille, and *Interior after Dinner*, 1868/69 (National Gallery of Art, Washington), with Camille and other adults, probably Alfred Sisley and his future wife Marie Lescouezec.

In *The Luncheon* the figures are rendered in a painterly style between realism and Impressionism. Camille may have posed for the seated woman and the woman leaning against the window, who does not appear to be with the group at the table. She is dressed for the outdoors with hat and gloves. The eye is drawn to details of the room's interior, the lace curtains at the window, the brilliant white tablecloth, and many objects including Jean's doll and ball on the floor. The doll appears again in *Jean Monet Sleeping*, 1868 (Ny Carlsberg Glyptotek, Copenhagen).

The Luncheon was rejected by the Paris Salon in 1870 as was Monet's *La Grenouillère*. Monet later exhibited *The Luncheon* in the first Impressionist exhibition in 1874. He had returned to the theme of a family repast in *The Luncheon*, c. 1873 (Musée d' Orsay, Paris), another large painting produced at a time when Monet was more secure financially and had a permanent residence and servants. Ten years on, another luncheon scene, *Luncheon beneath the Canopy*, 1883 (Private Collection), set in Monet's garden in Giverny and featuring Alice Hoschedé Monet, remained unfinished.

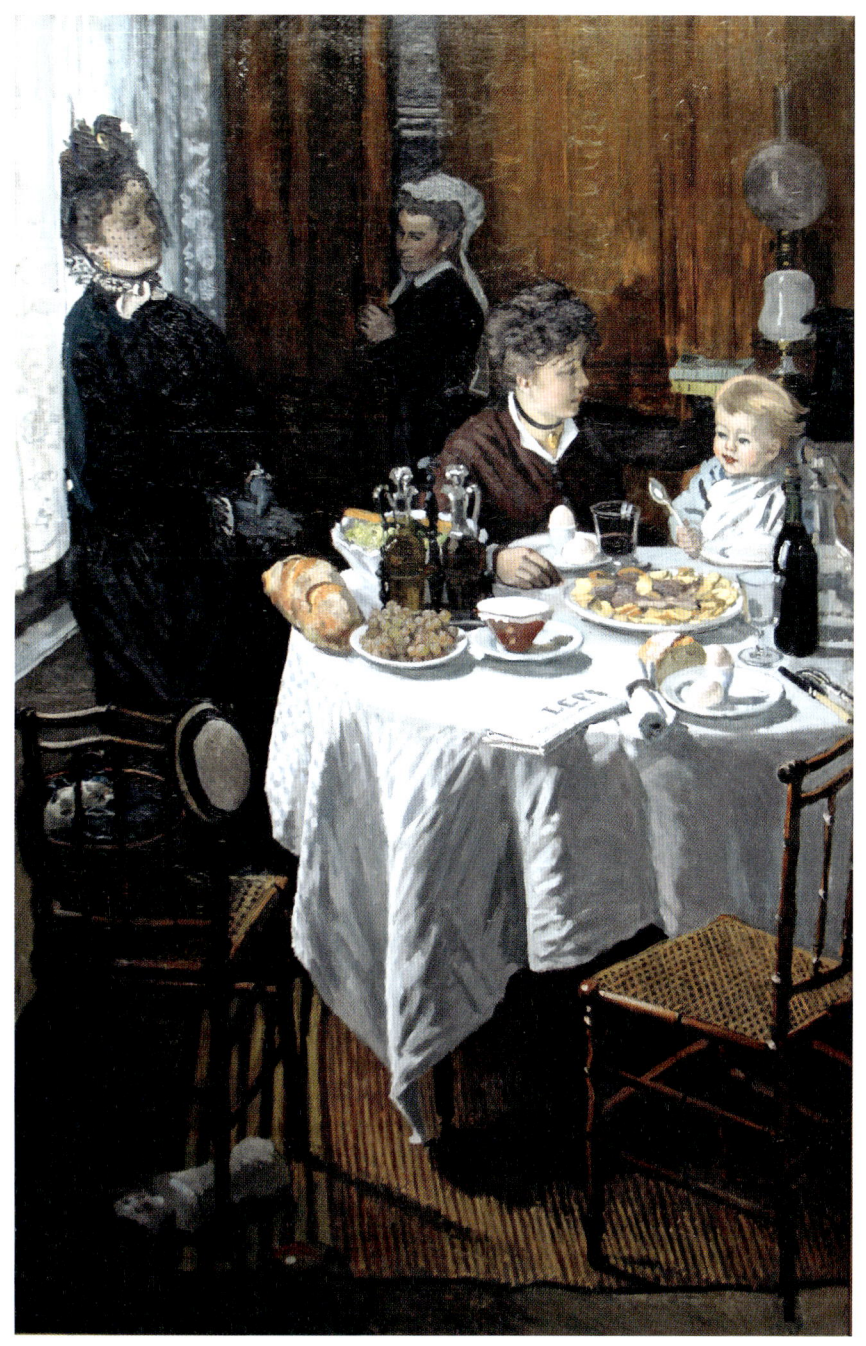

The Magpie, 1868/69

Oil on canvas
89 × 130 cm
Musée d'Orsay, Paris

In the winter of 1868 Louis-Joachim Gaudibert, a loyal patron of Monet's, arranged for a house near Étretat where Monet could have Camille and their infant son with him. Now with a proper home, Monet could paint winter scenes, including *The Magpie*.
The painting depicts a snowy scene in cold but fine dry weather with a weak-warm sun brightening the winter day. Monet's first painting of snow, *A Cart on a Snowy Road at Honfleur*, c. 1867 (Musée d'Orsay, Paris), pictured a man seated on his horse-drawn wooden cart travelling along a road covered with brilliant white dense snow. The cart was a focal point but the snow was the real subject matter. In *The Magpie* a heavy blanket of crisp and brilliantly white snow covers the fields. There are houses in the middle distance and a view of distant hills. A lone magpie perches on a wooden gate, its black, white and blue feathers clearly visible. It is surveying the snow-covered ground, perhaps looking for food. What stands out in this work is the composition's realism, the shadows in luminous, bluish-grey tones. Monet painted outdoors, observing the colours of the natural world and capturing them on canvas with ivory white, silver white, black, blue and burnt sienna.
Monet was known for sitting hours in freezing weather, wrapped up in layers of clothing and a thick coat and hat, determined to achieve exactly what he had in mind. One art critic commented on Monet's perseverance in freezing weather, when it was cold enough "to split rocks". On coming across him in Honfleur, "We glimpsed a little heater, then an easel, then a gentleman swathed in three overcoats, with gloved hands, his face half frozen. It was M. Monet, studying an aspect of the snow." *The Magpie* is one of some 140 snowscapes Monet painted, many under such conditions. This work was rejected by the 1869 Paris Salon, but the art critic Félix Fénéon (1861–1944) recognized its quality. Monet exhibited it at the Salon des Refusés that same year.

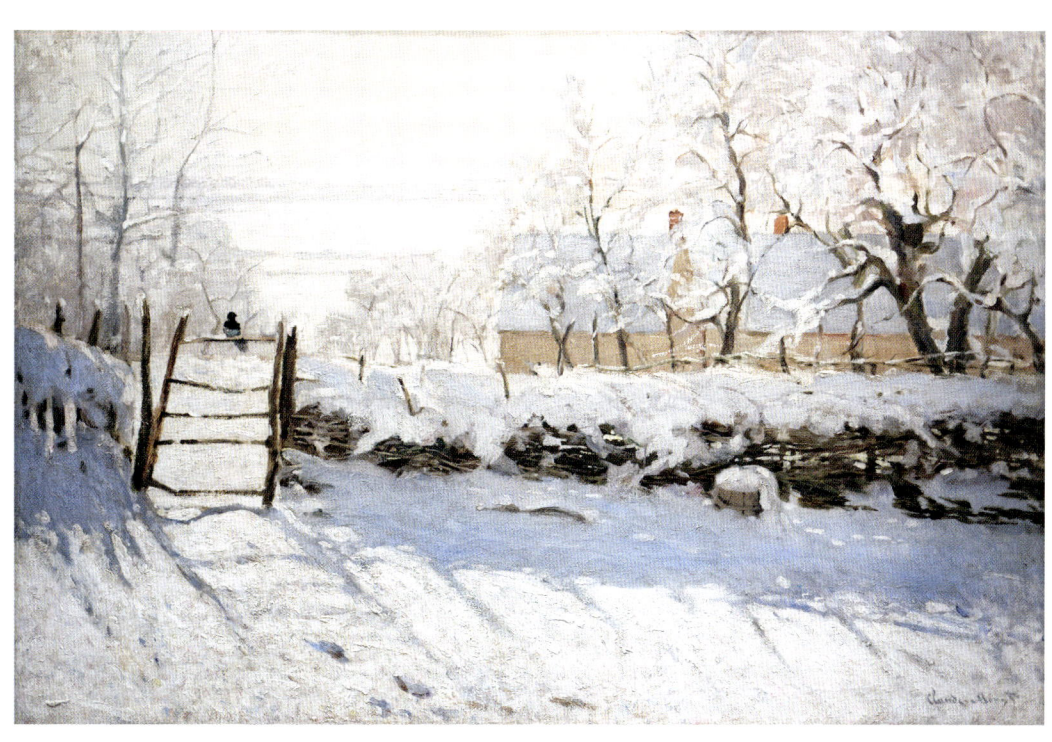

Camille on the Beach in Trouville, 1870

Oil on canvas
38.1 × 46.4 cm
Yale University Art Gallery, New Haven, Collection of Mr. and Mrs. John Hay Whitney,
B.A. 1926, Hon. 1956

By the middle of the century the Normandy seaside resort village Trouville-sur-Mer
had become a popular tourist destination. In 1870 Monet painted eight canvases there,
Camille posing for at least four of them. This one pictures her in three-quarter view,
seated in a chair on the sand on a blustery day. She wears a see-through veil and holds
her parasol against the wind as the choppy waves of the English Channel break behind
her. Now in her early twenties, she looks quite youthful. The lightweight fabric of her
dress has been painted with loose brushstrokes. The smaller figure of a woman is seen
standing in the breakers a short distance down the beach and a young boy with her is
daring a wave to catch him. On closer inspection one sees that their faces are
featureless.

In the middle distance a row of swimmers are standing in the water and far behind
them there are boats on the horizon. Some of the painting ground is visible, standing
in for clouds at the top right and around the figure of Camille. Perhaps Monet was
experimenting. He worked with neutral colours and soft pastels.

Most of the Trouville paintings feature sandy beaches, boardwalks and hotels, all
tourist attractions. Only with the pair of anglers pictured in the superb *Breakwater at
Trouville, Low Tide, 1870* (Szépmüvészti Múzeum, Budapest), did Monet suggest the
quieter fishing village of the past. The work's simplicity reflects the influence of
Japanese prints. It is of interest to compare these paintings with Monet's *Meditation,
or Madame Monet Sitting on a Sofa*, ca. 1871 (Musée d'Orsay, Paris), a highly realistic
canvas painted in London a few months later. Monet's compositions from this period
alternate elements of realism and Impressionism, depending on the effect he wanted
to achieve. This is evident in the earlier *Saint Germain l'Auxerrois*, 1867 (Alte
Nationalgalerie, Staatliche Museen zu Berlin), and *Garden of the Princess, Louvre*, 1867
(Allen Memorial Art Museum, Oberlin College, Ohio), both painted from the colonnade
of the Louvre.

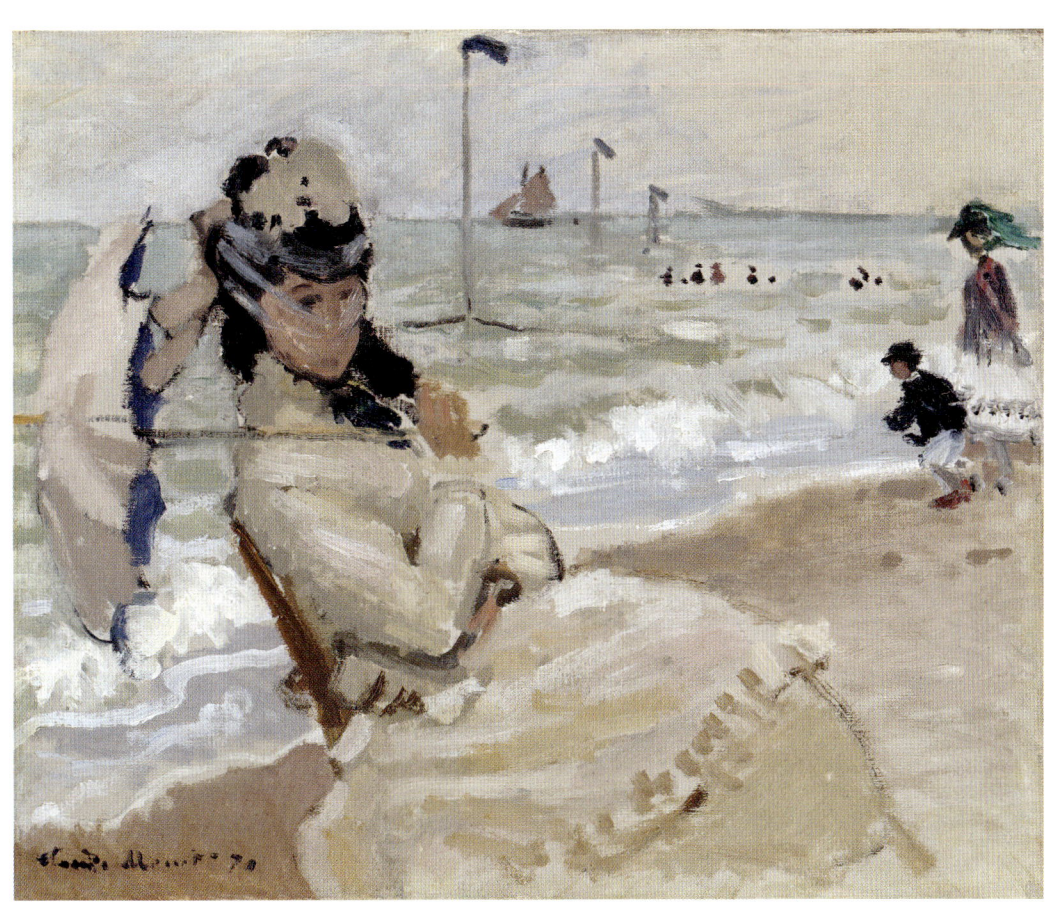

Meditation, or Madame Monet Sitting on a Sofa, 1871

Oil on canvas
48.2 × 74.5 cm
Musée d'Orsay, Paris

Camille Monet, sitting in repose on a low sofa, holds a closed book in her hands. The composition suggests that she has been reading and stopped to think about what she has read or perhaps the day ahead. Monet has captured that particular moment superbly. Camille was around twenty-four when Monet posed her for this work. They were living in a rented apartment in Kensington, London. The style of painting is less impressionistic, instead depicting the room and the sitter in a more realistic manner. The deep red tones of the sofa's loose floral cover, the rich red patterned carpet and the book are contrasted with the neutral wall and sheer curtains. This work was painted after the couple had stayed in Trouville, where paintings of Camille were rendered in almost luminous quick, broad brushstrokes recording a split second of time. There her facial features were indistinct, in contrast to the precision with which they are rendered here. Monet is exacting, perhaps in order to give the seated woman a narrative through objects and clothing, from the marble fireplace and ceramic vase and Japanese fan on the mantelpiece to her midnight-blue patterned dress, her shoes and red ribbon tied around her neck. Was Monet considering his viewers? Who might buy the painting? The work was exhibited as *Repose* at the *International Exhibition* in South Kensington in 1871 and catalogued as *An Interior* at the *Rouen Municipal Exhibition* in March-April 1872, but it remained in Monet's collection until purchased by Paul Durand-Ruel in 1873. At the time Monet painted it he had just met the French art dealer in London, both of them having escaped the fighting during the Franco-Prussian War. Durand-Ruel, who exhibited *Breakwater at Trouville, Low Tide* in his London gallery, liked Monet's work and may have shown other paintings as well, but his stock records from this period are scant.

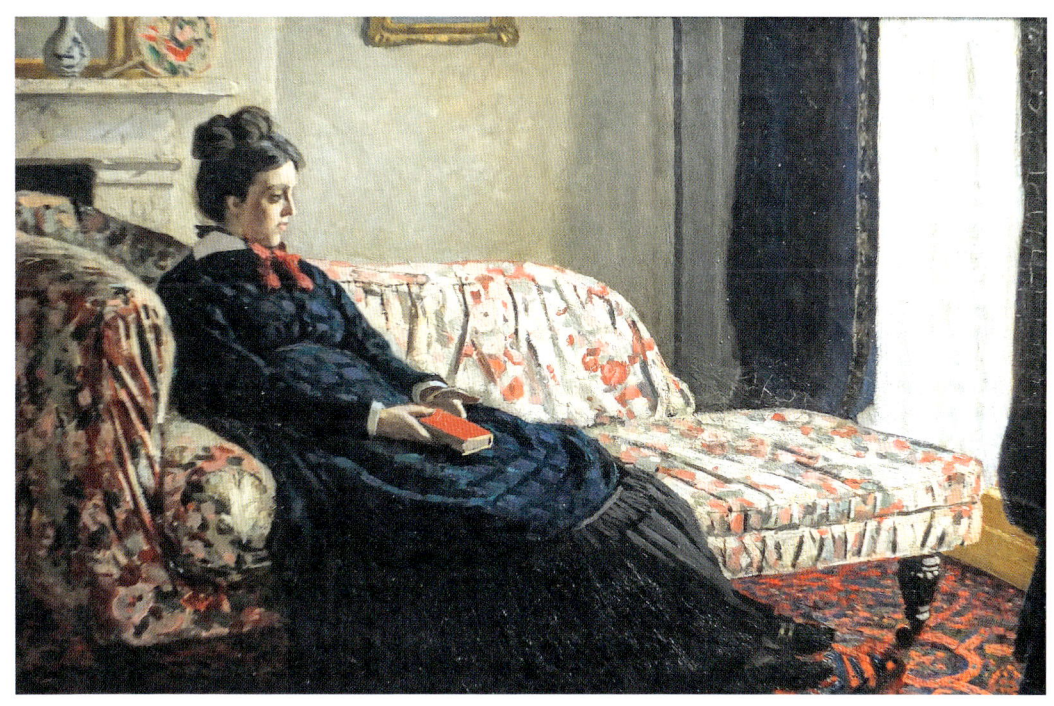

Houses by the Bank of the River Zaan, 1871/72

Oil on canvas
47.7 × 73.7 cm
Städel Museum, Frankfurt am Main

Before returning to France from England following his exile of nine months owing to the Franco-Prussian War Monet visited the Netherlands. With Camille and their young son Jean he stayed for several months in Zaandam, a town with around 12,000 inhabitants near Amsterdam. It is almost completely surrounded by water. He may have been urged to stop in Holland by Camille Pissarro or the Dutch painter Johan Jongkind, his former mentor, or even Charles Daubigny, with whom he had spent time in London. Camille occupied herself by giving lessons in conversational French to the locals. In their free time Monet visited the Rijksmuseum in Amsterdam and together they shopped for Delftware blue-and-white pots for their home, wherever it would be. Monet had sold two paintings in London and had the money to pay for accommodation and living expenses.

Houses by the Bank of the River Zaan was painted soon after their arrival. He chose a river scene in which to feature the Dutch houses built along its banks. Monet may have painted it from the river. He was interested in the local architecture, the houses with curving gables and painted a pale green with almost emerald-green shutters. The houses stood on the east bank of the Zaan. Monet's palette was controlled, the surrounding trees and water repeating the greens and browns of the buildings. His way of painting water follows that of *La Grenouillère*, 1869 (The Metropolitan Museum of Art, New York), where small, soft worm-like shapes in alternating shades of blue, green and white create the effect of free-flowing river water. Two women can be seen in the distance, lending scale to the composition. Monet painted multiple landscapes in and around Zaandam featuring the many windmills with their coloured sails. Two of them are the *Windmills near Zaandam*, 1871 (The Walters Art Museum, Baltimore), and *Windmill at Zaandam*, 1871 (Ny Carlsberg Glyptotek, Copenhagen).

He must have enjoyed his stay, for he wrote to Pissarro: "One would be busy for an entire painter's life." There was so much to paint that appealed to his lifelong interest in depicting water. While in Zaandam Monet, Camille and Jean posed for photographic portraits. Although Camille posed for more than fifty Monet paintings, photographs of her are rare. They returned to Paris in the autumn of 1871.

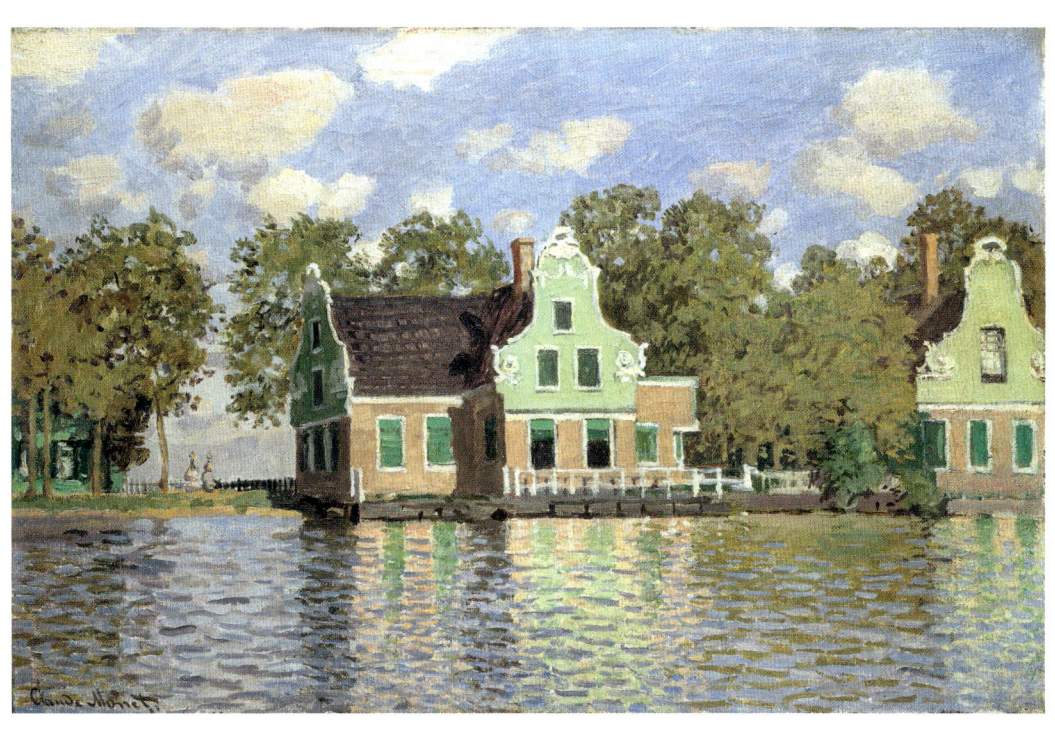

Impression, Sunrise, 1872

Oil on canvas
48 × 63 cm
Musée Marmottan Monet, Paris

This is the painting that so offended one critic when it was shown at the first
exhibition of the Société anonyme in 1874 that he mockingly dubbed the entire
show a group of "impressions".

Monet had painted it two years before in his hometown Le Havre, in Normandy.
He regularly returned there to paint local scenes. This was one of many works
from his early thirties that he first blocked out outdoors then finished in his studio.
The small painting pictures the rising sun over the port of Le Havre, its reflection
caught in the rippling water – a scene Monet must have witnessed time and again
since childhood. Through the haze one can see smokestacks belching smoke in
the distance. In the middle distance two small boats are silhouetted against the
reflection of the colourful sky. The simplicity of the composition recalls that of the
Japanese prints Monet admired, also the art of his tutor Jongkind and paintings
by the English artist J.M.W. Turner that Monet had studied in London in 1871.
Today the painting represents more than its content; it stands as an important
landmark in the history of art. It highlights the struggle of French painters in the
second half of the nineteenth century, primarily in and around Paris, to get their art
seen and sold. It marks the beginning of a decreasing focus on the traditions of the
Académie des Beaux-Arts and the structures of the annual Paris Salon. One has to
admire the artists Manet, Monet, Renoir, Pissarro, Caillebotte, and many more who
believed in painting the lighting effects on everyday scenes and how they were
affected by them. The painting was sold through Durand-Ruel in May 1874 to the
collector Ernest Hoschedé for 800 francs.

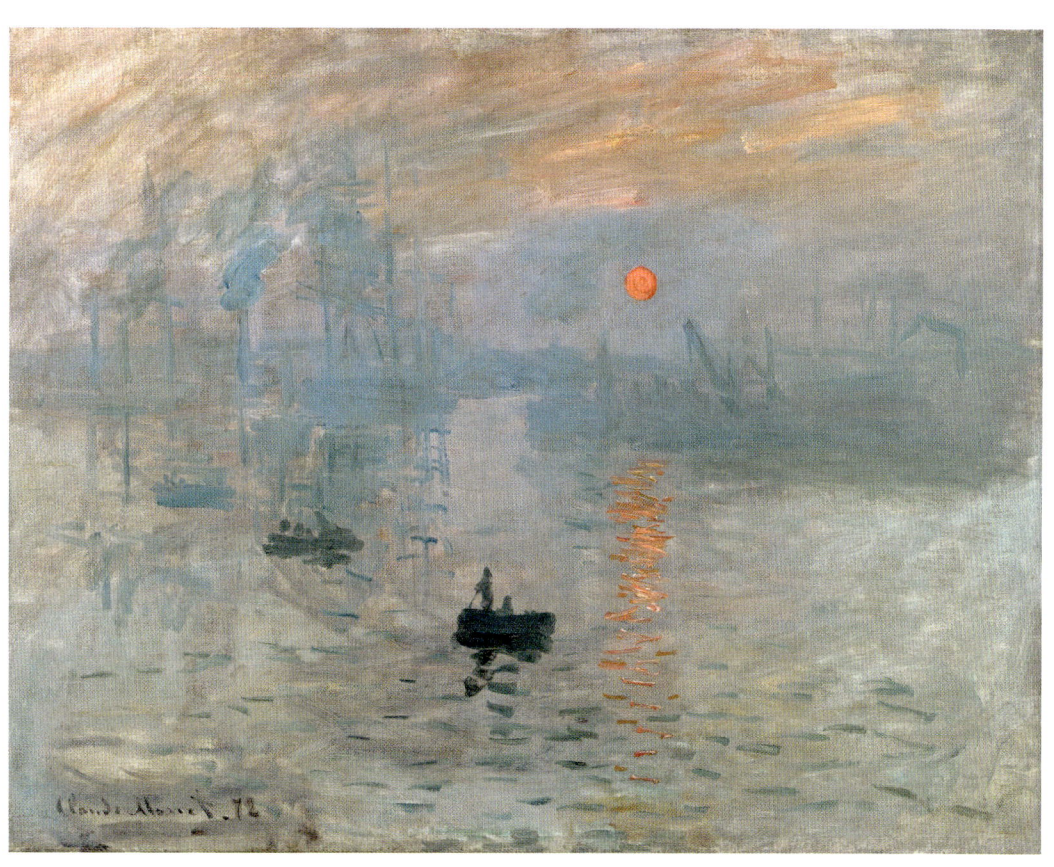

Still Life with Melon, ca. 1872

Oil on canvas
53 × 73 cm
Museu Calouste Gulbenkian, Lisbon

This painting dates from the same year as Monet's notorious *Impression, Sunrise*.
It too conveys his impression of a selected group of objects. There was a good
market for still lifes. Although considered the lowest in the hierarchy of academic
genres, the still life was extremely popular with the general public.
Still Life with Melon focuses on a table partly covered with a crisp white cloth and
seen slightly from above. On the left a Chinese blue-and-white dish is propped
against the wall and in front of it a decorative blue-and-white bowl resting on a
smaller plate is filled with peaches. Monet was a collector of Chinese porcelain.
To the right of the bowl of peaches is a large plate holding a ripe Charentais melon
that has been cut into large segments ready to be shared. In front of the melon lie
two bunches of ripe sweet green grapes. The painting relies on the complementary
colours orange and blue, set off by the green of the grapes and the mottled melon
rind and the deep red of some of the peaches. Monet used a white tablecloth and
Chinese porcelain in other still lifes, including the earlier *Still Life with Flowers and
Fruit*, 1869 (The J. Paul Getty Museum, Los Angeles), and *Still Life, Tea Service*, 1872
(Dallas Museum of Art).
In the latter we see the same tablecloth, its wove pattern and the ironed folds
accentuated. In addition to the blue-and-white tea service on a red lacquer tray
there is a sage plant potted in another Chinese bowl, its velvety-soft leaves perfectly
rendered. One is struck by Monet's ability to render textures, from the gleaming
metal of the spoon to the shiny porcelain to the pattern in the damask cloth and
the sage leaves.
Both *Still Life with Melon* and *Still Life, Tea Service* were exhibited at Durand-Ruel's
Paris gallery in November 1872. The melon still life sold immediately, but the other
one languished for some time before a buyer was found. It later featured in the first
Impressionist exhibition in New York in 1886.

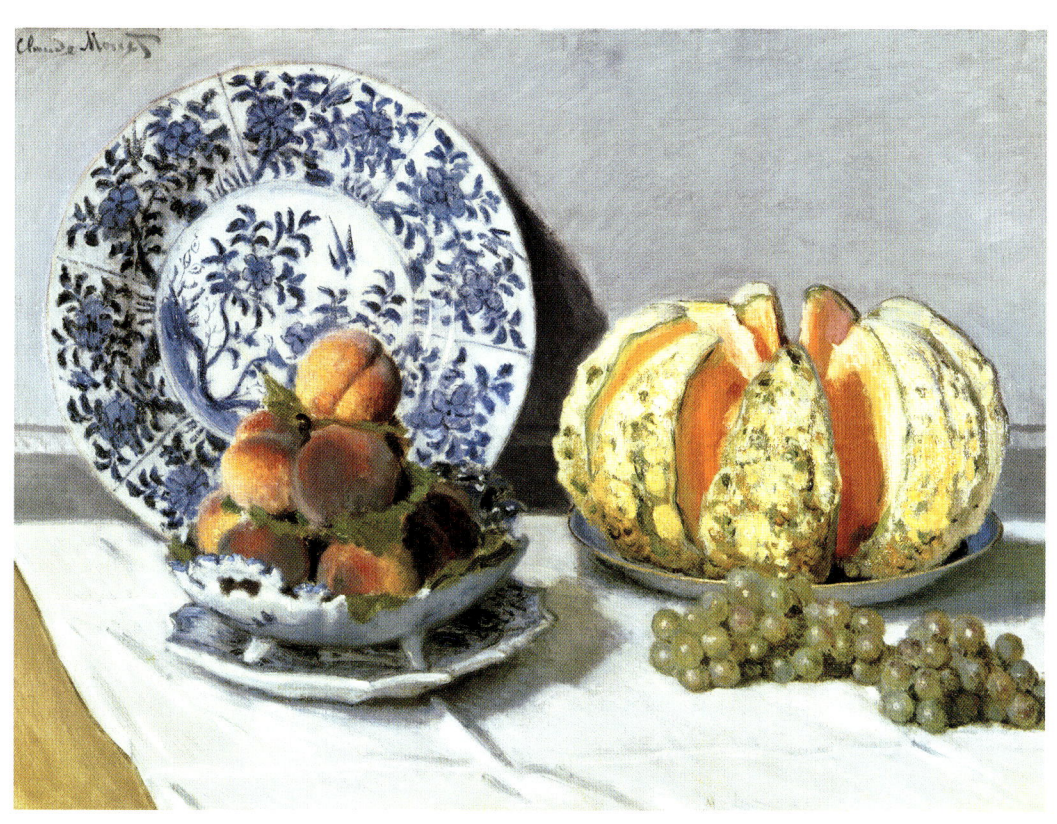

Le Boulevard des Capucines, 1873

Oil on canvas
61 × 80 cm
Pushkin Museum, St Petersburg

Stéphane Mallarme once said that one should "paint not the thing, but the effect that it creates." Monet certainly did so in his two versions of this view looking toward the Place de l'Opera. Both were painted from an upper window at 35 Boulevard des Capucines, on the corner of Rue Daunou, where the photographer Nadar had a studio. The one shown here is considered to be the version shown at the first Impressionist exhibition in 1874. It is an aerial view of the busy street below.

The other work is a vertical composition in the Nelson-Atkins Museum of Art, Kansas City. That version also includes the row of trees dividing the boulevard and its line of horse-drawn carriages waiting for a fare. Many people throng the streets. Of interest is a top-hatted figure who leans out of a window at right on the same level as the artist, also contemplating the scene below. It is a grey day in winter or early spring, for the trees are bare. Monet used a monotone palette highlighted by a splash of pink provided by the seller of balloons in the foreground. The painting was sold in 1875.

The Pushkin Museum version pictures the same scene in a horizontal format more densely populated with pedestrians. A review of the 1874 Impressionist exhibition by Philippe Burty published in *The Academy*, a London periodical, included a favourable reference to *Le Boulevard des Capucines*. The review in *The Examiner* by the art critic Frederick Wedmore included a longer description of it with its "unresting crowd of foot passengers and carriages, crossing, mingling, going here, going there under the towering house-rows. … There is life and colour in it." Monet captured a moment when the street thronged with pedestrians on both sides. Half of the boulevard is bathed in bright sunshine while the other side lies in shadow. The sky is bluish above the buildings receding into the distance. At right, on the same level as the artist, two top-hatted men lean from a balcony to view the street below. This painting was sold in September 1874.

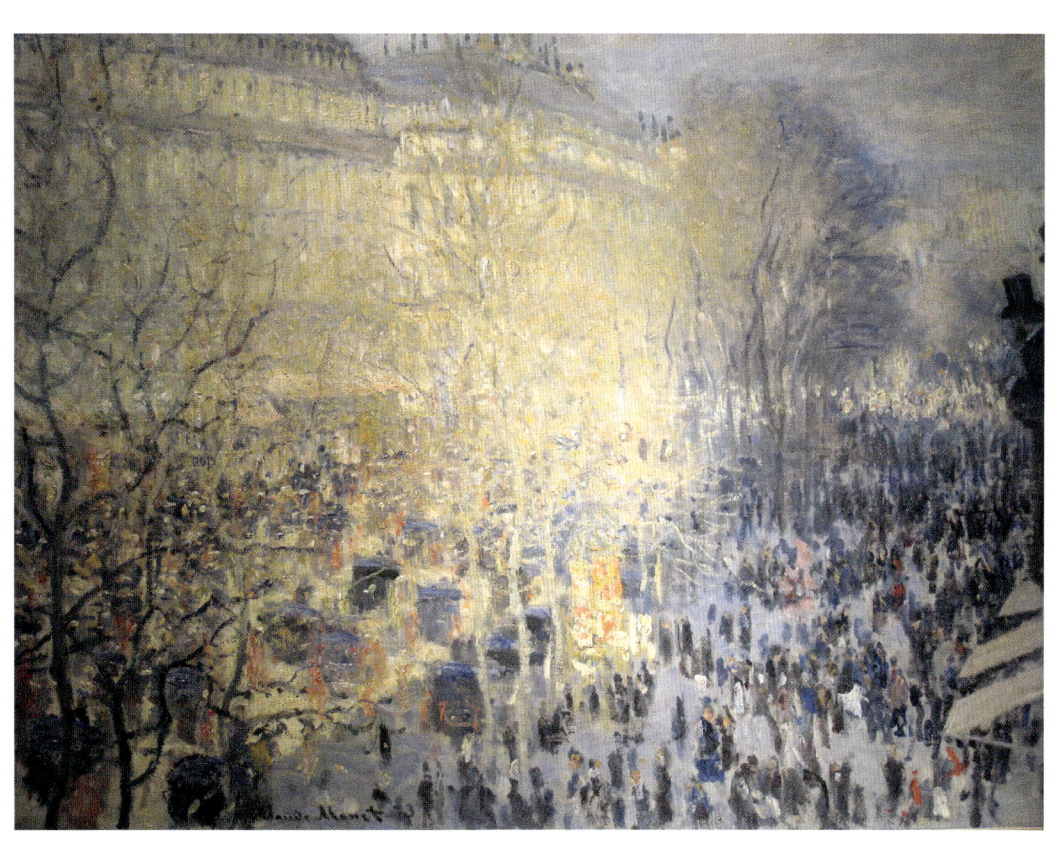

The Coalmen, ca. 1875

Oil on canvas
54 × 65.5 cm
Musée d'Orsay, Paris

The setting of this work is the suburb of Asnières on the river Seine, a brief train journey northwest of Paris. Monet included two road bridges for orientation. The iron bridge in the foreground has vehicles and pedestrians crossing it; in the distance is the Pont de Clichy. Below the nearer one coal porters are unloading heavy sacks of coal, possibly destined for the gas factory at Clichy, from coal barges lined up along the riverbank. Monet pictured the industrial landscape along the Seine as well. In the distance we glimpse factories with smoking chimneys – the burners of the coal.
The work's muted greenish greys are appropriate for a depiction of such monotonous labour. This is an industrial painting, not a leisurely scene by the river.
Monet exhibited this painting for sale at Paris's Hôtel Drouot on 24 March 1875, alongside works by Berthe Morisot, Alfred Sisley and Auguste Renoir, with whom he had organized a group show. Paul Durand-Ruel was the appraiser, Charles Pillet the auctioneer. Édouard Manet had asked the Le Figaro art critic to attend. It turned into a fiasco, with unknown people trying to interrupt the bidding. Durand-Ruel recalled the auctioneer's having summoned the police to avoid confrontations. The review by Le Figaro's art critic savaged the paintings that included Morisot's La chasse aux papillons, 1874 (Musée d'Orsay, Paris), and Renoir's Le Pont Neuf, 1872 (National Gallery of Art, Washington): "... The impression the Impressionists give is that of a cat walking on the keyboard of a piano, or a monkey grabbing a colour box. However, this may be a good deal for those who speculate on the art of the future." Some bids were so low that the artists bought back their own work. The Coalmen sold for 225 francs, and with his twenty works Monet enjoyed the best sales of the group. In his notebook he recorded a net profit of 2,825 francs.

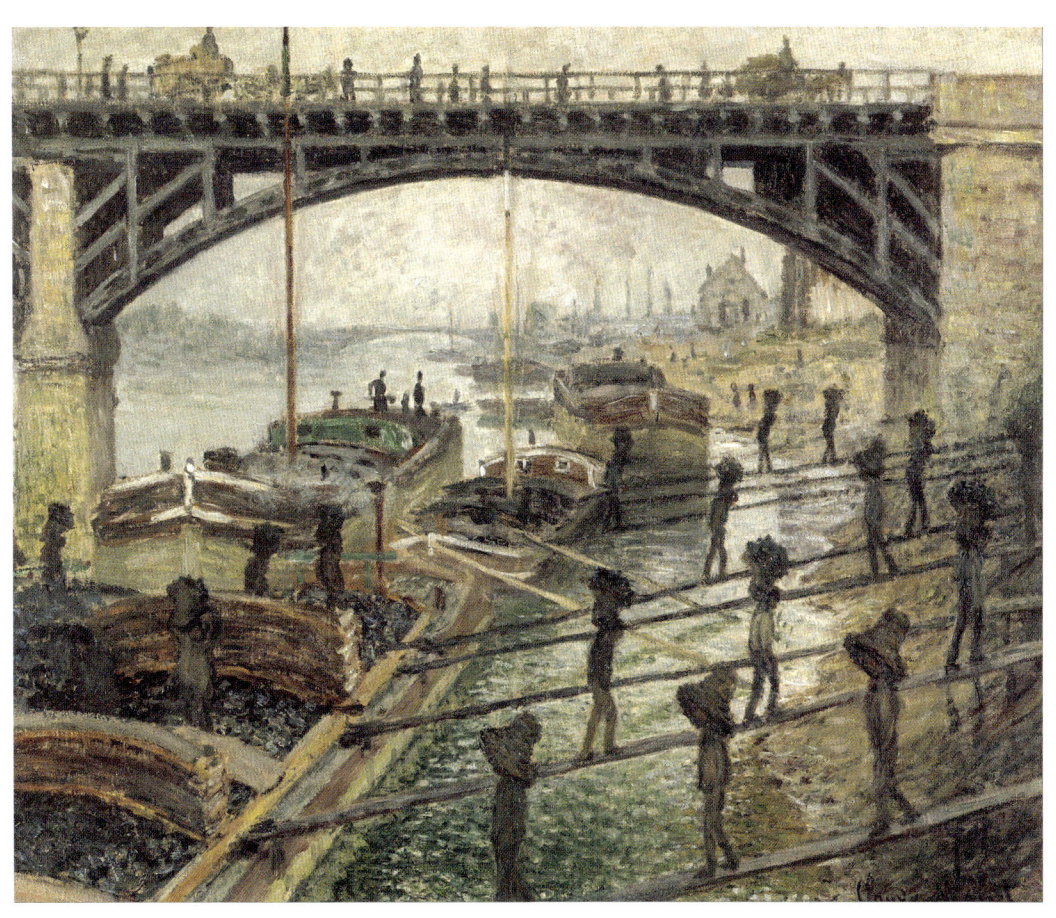

La Japonaise (Camille Monet in Japanese Costume), 1876

Oil on canvas
231.8 × 142.3 cm
Museum of Fine Arts, Boston

This is a life-size painting of Camille Monet theatrically dressed in a Japanese scarlet and gold kimono embroidered with the figure of a Kabuki warrior. Such figures were larger-than-life characters of Japanese theatre, their costumes highly decorative. Camille stands sideways, holding an open fan in front of her smiling face while turning to look at the viewer. Behind her is a wall display of sixteen decoratve *uchiwa*, Japanese paddle-shape fans. Camille wears a blond wig, to emphasise that she is European, a Parisienne dressing up as a Japanese woman. At this time Paris was in the grip of *Japonisme*, a craze for everything Japanese, from prints to porcelain, clothing, fans and peacock feathers, which appeared in art too. Monet owned several Japanese theatre costumes. This kimono might be one of them. According to the catalogue of the second Impressionist exhibition, held for a month in 1876 at Paul Durand-Ruel's house-gallery at 11 Rue le Peletier, the painting was created for a decorative wall panel.

In this show of 252 works each artist had his own submissions grouped together. The more avant-garde artists were placed toward the end of the exhibition, the less controversial ones at the beginning. Art critics were still sceptical. Albert Wolff, writing for *Le Figaro*, titled his review "Misfortune in the Rue le Peletier".

Camille Monet in Japanese Costume was listed by Monet as *Japonerie*, a term used to describe Western art imitating that of Japan. It was mistitled *La Chinoise* by some art critics. One suggested that the composition had two heads, referring to the Kabuki warrior image close to Camille's thigh. It was a painting viewers loved or hated, but it caught their attention. The theatricality of it – including the mask-like maquillage – suggests that Camille delighted in theatre and acting. Monet loved Japanese prints and especially admired Edo-period Kabuki theatre art.

Monet exhibited eighteen paintings, including *La Japonaise*, the standout work in the show, which sold for 2,000 francs. The exhibition was a success; the artists were able to pay Durand-Ruel 3,000 francs for use of the gallery space and retain 1,500 francs each. Much later, when it was purchased by the art dealer Paul Rosenberg in 1918, Monet would refer to the *La Japonaise* as a "piece of junk," to his thinking of little artistic value.

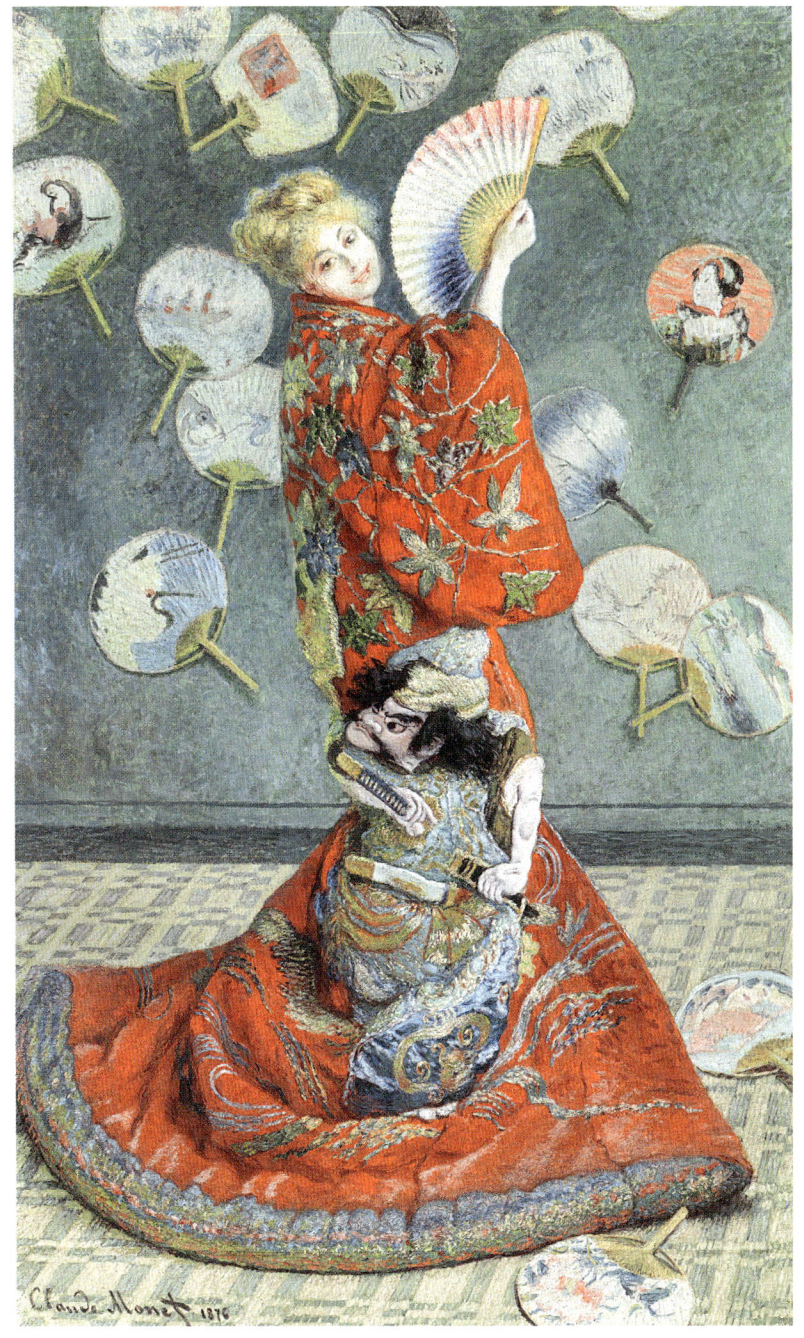

The Gare St-Lazare, 1877

Oil on canvas
54.3 × 73.6 cm
The National Gallery, London

Paris's railway stations and the steam locomotives they housed were symbols of the modern city being created by Baron Georges-Eugène Haussmann. The Saint-Lazare station was built in 1837, the first one in Paris. By 1870 it was accommodating eleven million passengers a year. It became a favourite subject for the Impressionist painters. Édouard Manet celebrated it in *The Railway* (*Gare St-Lazare*, 1873 (National Gallery of Art, Washington) featuring the painter Victorine Meurent posing as a nanny with a young child staring through railings at the smoke and tracks below.

Monet had known the station well since childhood, as that was where one caught trains to Normandy. Having left Argenteuil, he rented an apartment nearby in the rue d'Édimbourg. In January 1877 he contacted the station's director and gained permission to paint inside on a concourse by the railway tracks. Working on many canvases at once, hoping to capture the atmosphere at different times of day, he set up an easel on a station platform in the thick of the steam and smoke of the trains. Between January and March he produced a full twelve paintings and showed six or seven of them at the third Impressionist exhibition in April. By then the group officially styled themselves "Impressionists". That same year Gustave Caillebotte exhibited *Le Pont de l'Europe*, 1876/77 (Petit Palais, Geneva, Switzerland), a view of the bridge with a passerby looking down into the station. Monet painted the bridge as well; in his *Le Pont de l'Europe, Gare Saint-Lazare*, 1877 (Musée Marmottan Monet, Paris), it is depicted from the rail tracks below.

Monet's *Gare St-Lazare* depicts the interior of the station. It is one of the four Monet painted of this view. In this version his palette is virtually monochrome, which sets off the black locomotives and the iron framing of the shed's glass roof. Monet was looking from the platforms toward the shed's entrance, with trains on either side. At right are the three arched roofs of the parcel offices. Locomotive steam fills the air. A crowd of people is waiting to board. The inclusion of the iron-girder roof helps to indicate the station's size. In the distance we can see the iron Pont de l'Europe.

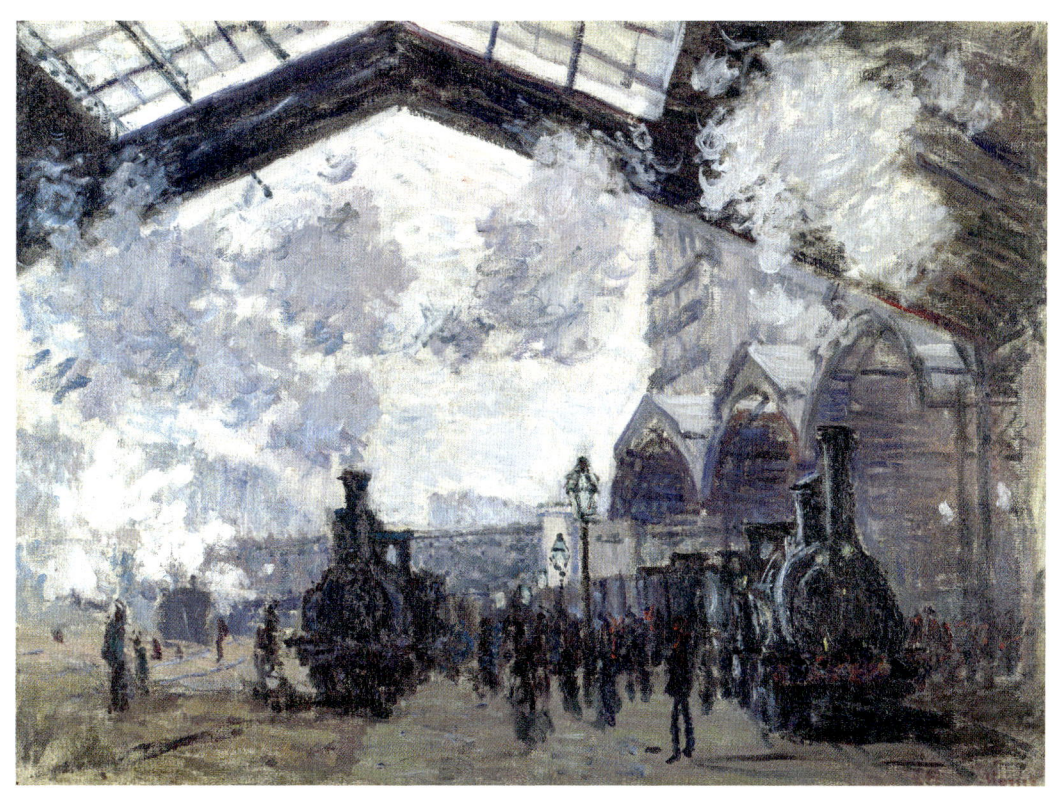

The Turkeys, 1877

Oil on canvas
174 × 172.5 cm
Musée d'Orsay, Paris

This painting was commissioned in 1876–77 by the art collector Ernest Hoschedé for the grand rotunda salon of his Château de Rottembourg in Montgeron, southeast of Paris. Hoschedé wanted four large panels depicting features of the château's grounds, leaving the choice up to Monet. The present one was a huge success, bringing the estate's gardens and domestic fowl into the château. It was painted from a low viewpoint, focusing on the birds as they ate and foraged in their accustomed surroundings. Their white plumage is in strong contrast to the rich green of the grass and trees. The placement of the birds, dominating the foreground to middle distance, leads the eye toward the vast pinkish-red walls of the château in the distance. *The Turkeys* was exhibited at the third Impressionist exhibition in 1877. It made some critics laugh, but more at the subject matter than at the method or style of painting.

The other paintings from this set are *A Corner of the Garden at Montgeron*, ca. 1876 (State Hermitage Museum, St Petersburg); *The Pond at Montgeron*, ca. 1876 (State Hermitage Museum, St Petersburg); and *The Hunt,* 1876 (Private Collection). The last named pictures a glorious autumn setting featuring Ernest Hoschedé and two other men with guns on a path in Montgeron with the day's downed game in the foreground. But was Monet the poacher? It was at this time that Monet and Alice Hoschedé became lovers.

Unfortunately, Hoschedé was forced to sell *The Turkeys* at auction at Paris's Hôtel Drouot in 1878 along with forty-eight other paintings – sixteen by Monet plus works by Morisot, Pissarro, Renoir and Sisley – as he had gone bankrupt. Monet must have regretted parting with *The Turkeys*. The painting came up for sale at Durand-Ruel's gallery in 1909. Monet wrote to the seller, Winnaretta Singer, Princess Edmond de Polignac, an American heiress who had bought the work in 1906. He expressed an interest in buying it but asssured her that the asking price, around 30 000 francs, was more than he wanted to pay. He was unable to secure a discount, as Singer decided to keep it for her new house in London. It remained in her collection until it was bequeathed to the Louvre in 1947.

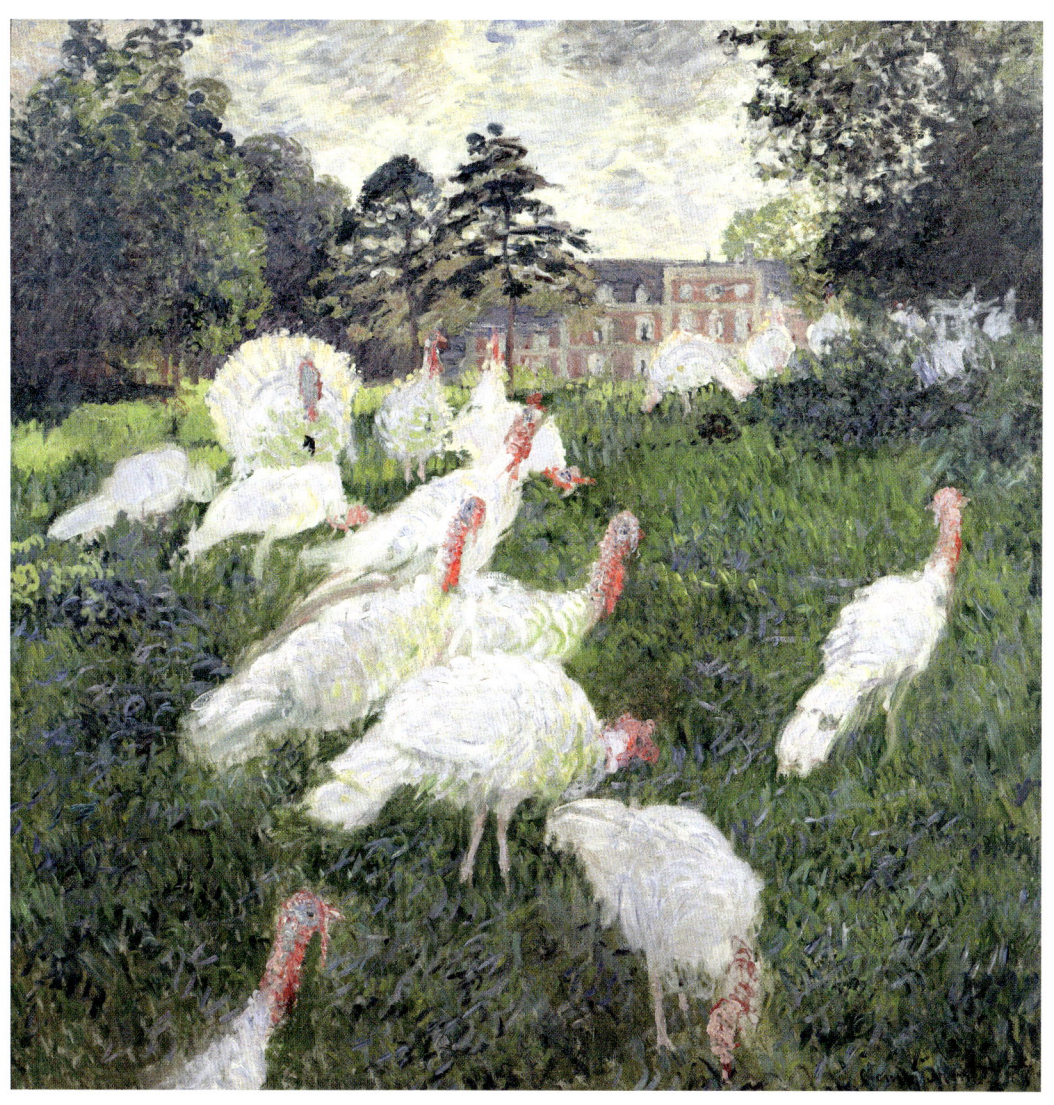

Apples and Grapes, 1879/80

Oil on canvas
67.6 × 89.5 cm
The Metropolitan Museum of Art, New York

On the death of Camille, his model, muse and lover since 1865 and wife since 1870, Monet was grief-stricken. The father of two young children, he was suddenly faced with the reality of his parental responsibilities. In the next few months he concentrated on his home life. He already had a live-in mistress, Alice Hoschedé, and her six children but he missed his wife.

While he adjusted to a new life, he devoted his painting to still lifes like this one. Monet is not known for his works in the genre but his oeuvre includes many, dating from the 1850s. They reveal an awareness of Dutch still-life paintings, as in *Still Life with Pheasant*, ca. 1861 (Musée d'Orsay, Paris). Others from the early 1860s include one picturing a cut of raw beef and a garlic bulb, an atmospheric, realistic work titled *Still Life: The Quarter of Meat*, ca. 1864 (Musée d'Orsay, Paris), and *Still Life with Bottle, Carafe, Bread and Wine*, ca. 1862/63 (National Gallery of Art, Washington). In the latter the light refracted by the water carafe and the sharp edge of the butter on a plate show that Monet was attentive to every facet of a work. Fifteen years on, he had perfected his skill at portraying objects in a still life. In the present one a basket on a table overflows with autumn garden produce, two varieties of apples and both black and green grapes. The angle is low, to focus on the basket, the fruit and the white tablecloth laid across half the table. There is an element of Auguste Renoir's rich fusion of colour in this work, bringing a realism to the produce and the domestic setting.

In addition to still lifes he painted portraits of his children at this time, including *Portrait of Michel Monet as a Baby*, 1878/79 (Musée Marmottan Monet, Paris); *Portrait of Jean Monet*, 1880 (Musée Marmottan Monet, Paris), in which he looks wide-eyed and wistful; and *Michel Monet in a Pompom Hat*, 1880 (Musée Marmottan Monet, Paris). He painted portraits of Alice Hoschedé's children too, his portraits and still lifes providing glimpses of his extended family and his domestic life.

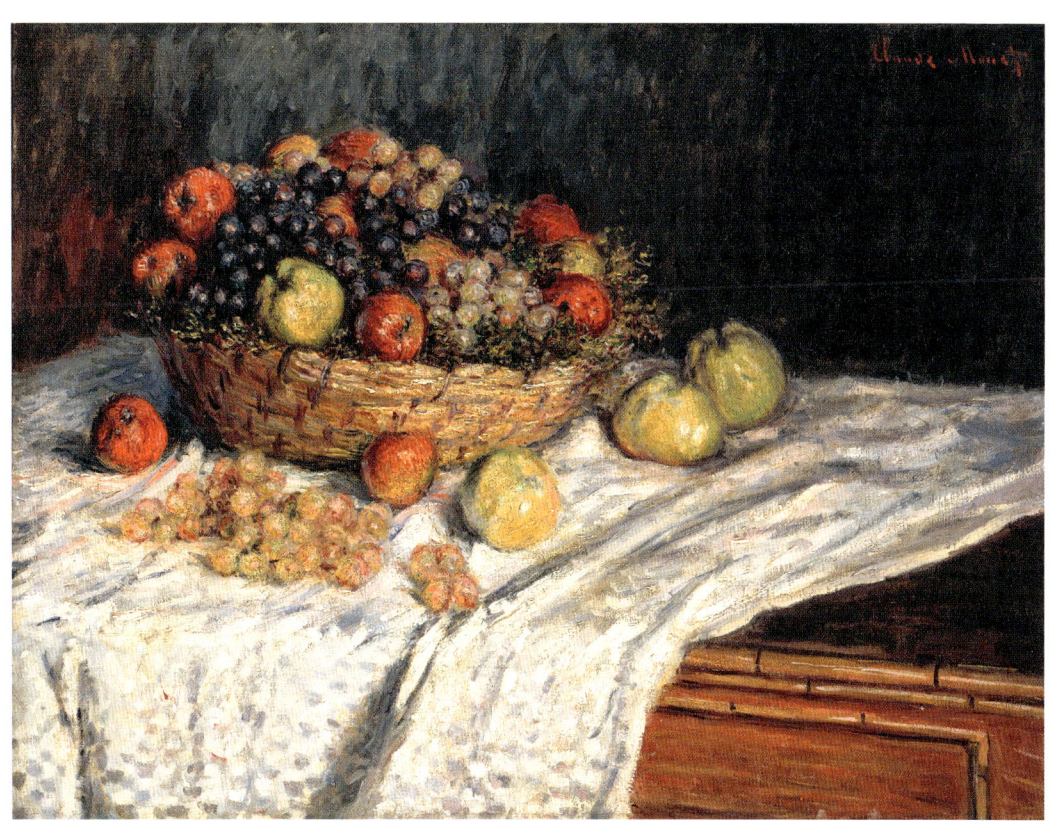

The Artist's Garden at Vétheuil, 1881

Oil on canvas
151.5 × 121 cm
National Gallery of Art, Washington, Ailsa Mellon Bruce Collection

Monet had taken an interest in gardening and plants from an early age. Wherever he lived – most often in rented houses – a garden was integral to his way of life and painting. In 1878 he rented a house on a bend in the river Seine in Vétheuil, 40 miles northwest of Paris. With the landlord's permission he landscaped the terraces of the garden and planted them abundantly. The Monets shared their house with the recently bankrupted Ernest Hoschedé's family, including his wife Alice and their six children. *The Artist's Garden at Vétheuil* was painted after Monet's wife Camille had died in this house in 1879. The boy with the wagon is Monet's young son, and on the steps behind him are other members of his extended household. The woman at the top of the steps is probably Alice. In the background we see the house on the right. The garden path leading down to the Seine is dappled with sunlight. The plum-coloured shadows on it suggest warm, sunny weather. The tall sunflowers on either side of the steps are a riotous mix of sun-yellow and burnt orange tones. They tower above the young children on the path and the steps. The blue-and-white ceramic pots that line the path belonged to Monet; he took them with him whenever he moved and they appear in several paintings.

A similar view without people that accentuates the sunflowers is *The Steps at Vétheuil*, 1881 (Private Collection). Monet created four versions of this composition. While Ernest Hoschedé stayed in Paris, avoiding creditors and the bailiffs who called at the Vétheuil house, Alice – replacing Camille – posed for numerous paintings. *The Terrace at Vétheuil*, 1881 (Private Collection), and *Alice Hoschedé in the Garden*, 1881 (Private Collection), show how beautiful the garden was.

Monet's paintings from Vétheuil picture all aspects of his surroundings, including the view of Lavacourt across the river from the bottom of his garden through the garden gate. *The Garden Gate at Vétheuil*, 1881 (Private Collection), and *Flowers at Vétheuil*, 1881 (Private Collection), picture an abundance of colourful plantings framing a view of Lavacourt's buildings on the opposite bank.

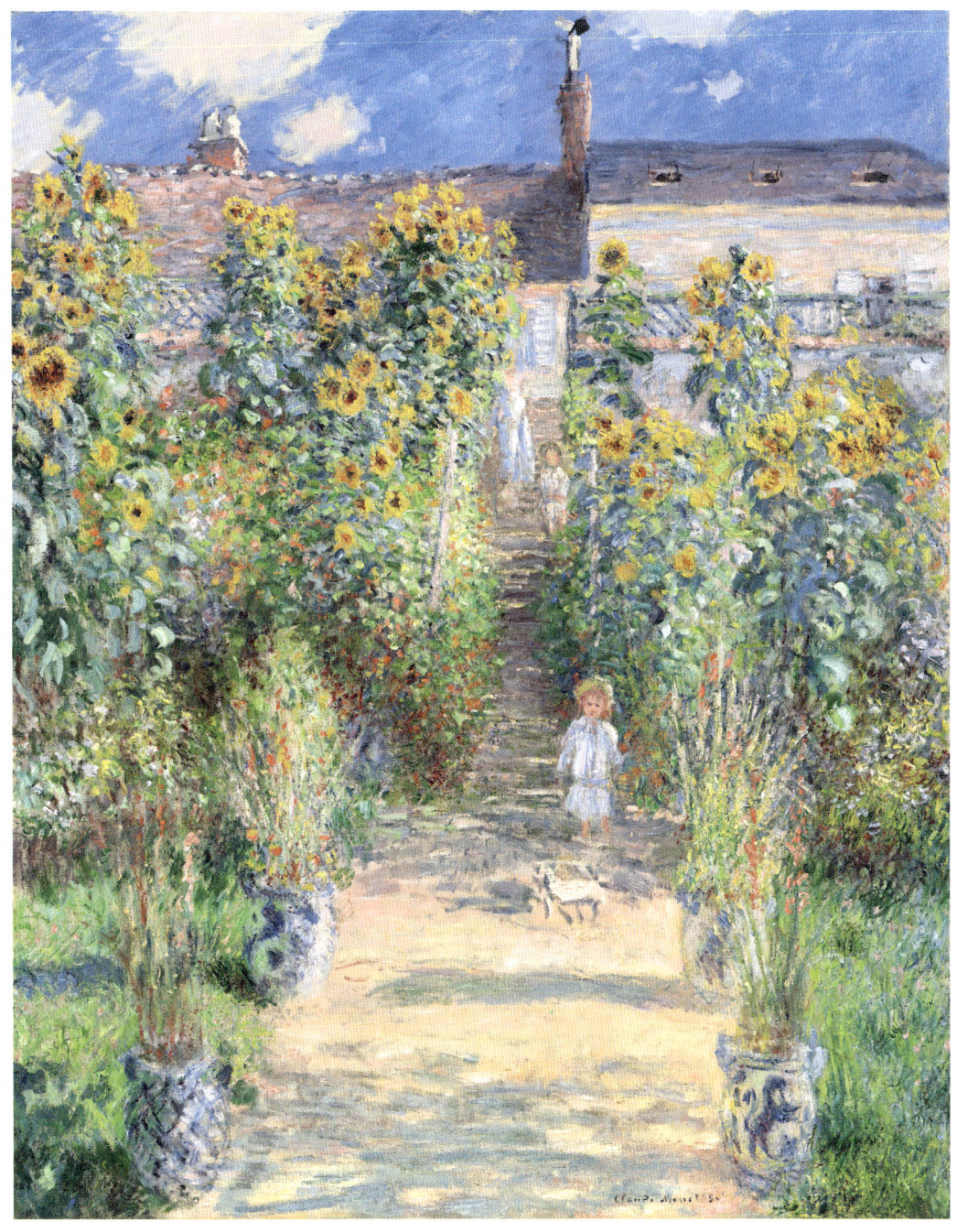

Field of Poppies,1881

Oil on canvas
58 × 79 cm
Museum Boijmans Van Beuningen, Rotterdam

Monet painted many varied compositions of poppy fields, often along the Seine at the hamlet of Lavacourt near Vétheuil, at Argenteuil and Giverny. An early work, *Poppy Field*, 1873 (Musée d'Orsay, Paris), featured his wife Camille and young son Jean walking through a field of vibrant red poppies. Eight years on, his 1881 *Field of Poppies*, painted in the plain of Lavacourt, shows how his brushwork had altered. Here the poppy blooms are short red dashes. The colour creates the mass of poppies in a landscape that stretches into the distance, a lone tree adding perspective. Monet explained that the poppies in this work were simply "small, sharply placed strokes". To explain his approach, his advice was: "Try to forget what objects you have before you – a tree, a house, a field, or whatever. Merely think ›Here is a little square of blue, here an oblong of pink, here a streak of yellow‹, and paint it just as it looks to you, the exact colour and shape, until it gives you your own impression of the scene before you." Around the same time he painted *Lavacourt under Snow* (The National Gallery, London), a vision of blue shadows on white crunchy snow banked up against the low houses at right and a pinkish glow on the distant, sunlit hills, all captured in wide brushstrokes. At this time Monet was staying at Vétheuil on the Seine, opposite Lavacourt.

Vincent van Gogh (1853–90), Monet's younger contemporary, painted poppies while staying in Auvers sur Oise, in *Poppy Field*, 1890 (Kunstmuseum The Hague). The painting is a density of strong reds and greens. His painting of poppies was informed by Monet's *Field of Poppies*. Vincent's brother, the art dealer Theo van Gogh (1857–91), was a regular guest at Monet's house in Giverny. He bought many paintings, and brokered some of Monet's works in Paris. At times Monet favoured him over Durand-Ruel, possibly because he shared with artists the profit from sales. However, Monet sold this painting to Durand-Ruel in the autumn of 1881.

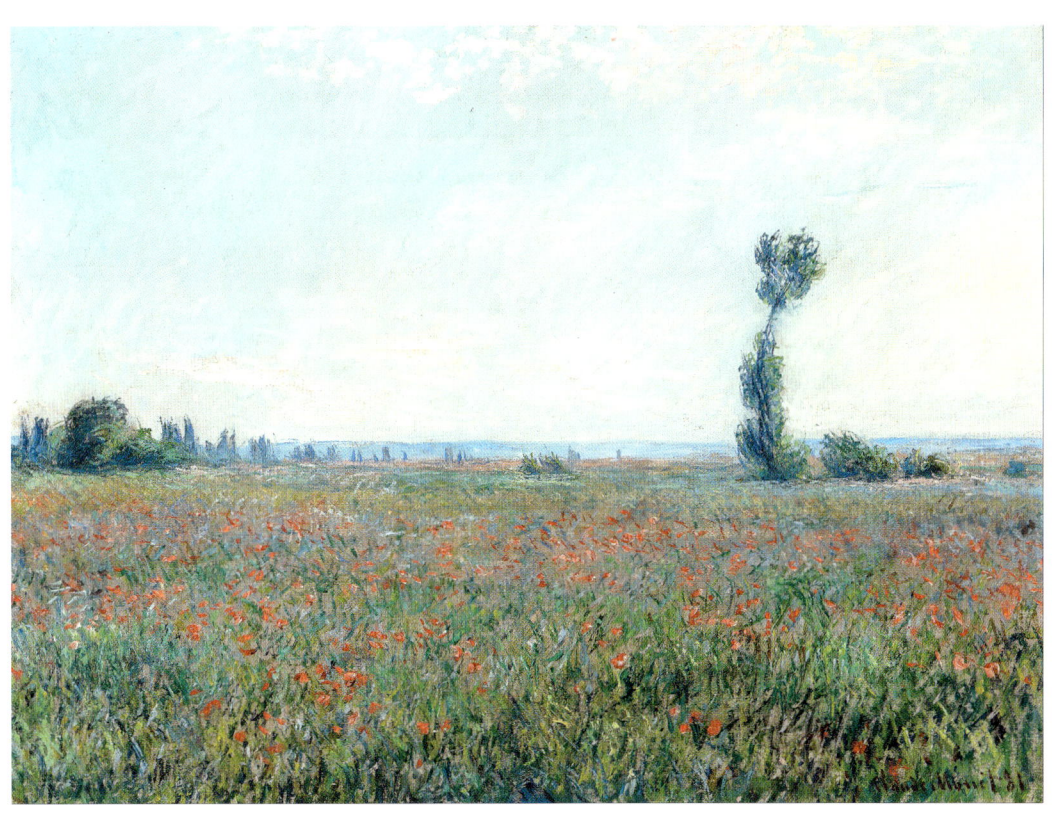

Bordighera, Italy, 1884

Oil on canvas
60 × 73 cm
Hasso Plattner Collection

When Monet visited Italy in January 1884 he had recently moved into a large house in
Giverny to accommodate his extended family. His finances were in good order. He had
sold many paintings and his art was being exhibited in multiple European cities.
A month before, Monet had joined his friend Auguste Renoir on a reconnaissance for
interesting locations. They visited Paul Cézanne (1839–1906) in L'Estaque, close to
Marseilles, then travelled by train along the French-Italian coast as far as Genoa.
They stopped in Bordighera along the way, "pure pine country" as Renoir recalled it.
It was a successful painting trip. In mid January 1884 Monet returned to Bordighera
alone, staying until early April. The town is situated in the coastal region close to the
French border between San Remo in Italy and Menton in France. In the 1880s it had
around 2,000 inhabitants plus many English, German, and French tourists arriving by
rail, attracted by the good hotels, a microclimate that produced warmer winters, and
its natural beauty. It was a perfect winter resort with easy access by train since 1878.
During his stay Monet took trips out to different locations, once trekking into the
mountains with English painters to Dolceacqua. He considered the coast a "fairyland".
He painted a total of fifty-one canvases, which he had some difficulty getting through
border customs on his return to France.
Monet's *Bordighera, Italy* pictures a hilly landscape with the hilltop old town of
Città Alta di Bordighera. The view of the city, painted from the Torre dei Mostaccini, is
framed by a pair of pine trees that draw our gaze to the collection of red roofs and the
Ligurian Sea beyond. Monet is reported to have said "The motif is secondary to me;
what I want to paint is what there is between the motif and me." He looked for the
beauty of the light as his inspiration. In this work he portrays pale pink clouds in a hazy
blue sky, mirroring the deeper colours of the hills in shades of purple and deep pink.
His paintings in and around Bordighera reveal the atmosphere of the location and its
landscape. On his trips through the hills, noting the vast ravines, he painted a series
of views of Dolceacqua, painting its stunning arched bridge, as in *The Old Bridge on
the Nervia at Dolceacqua*, 1884 (Clark Art Institute, Williamstown, Mass.).

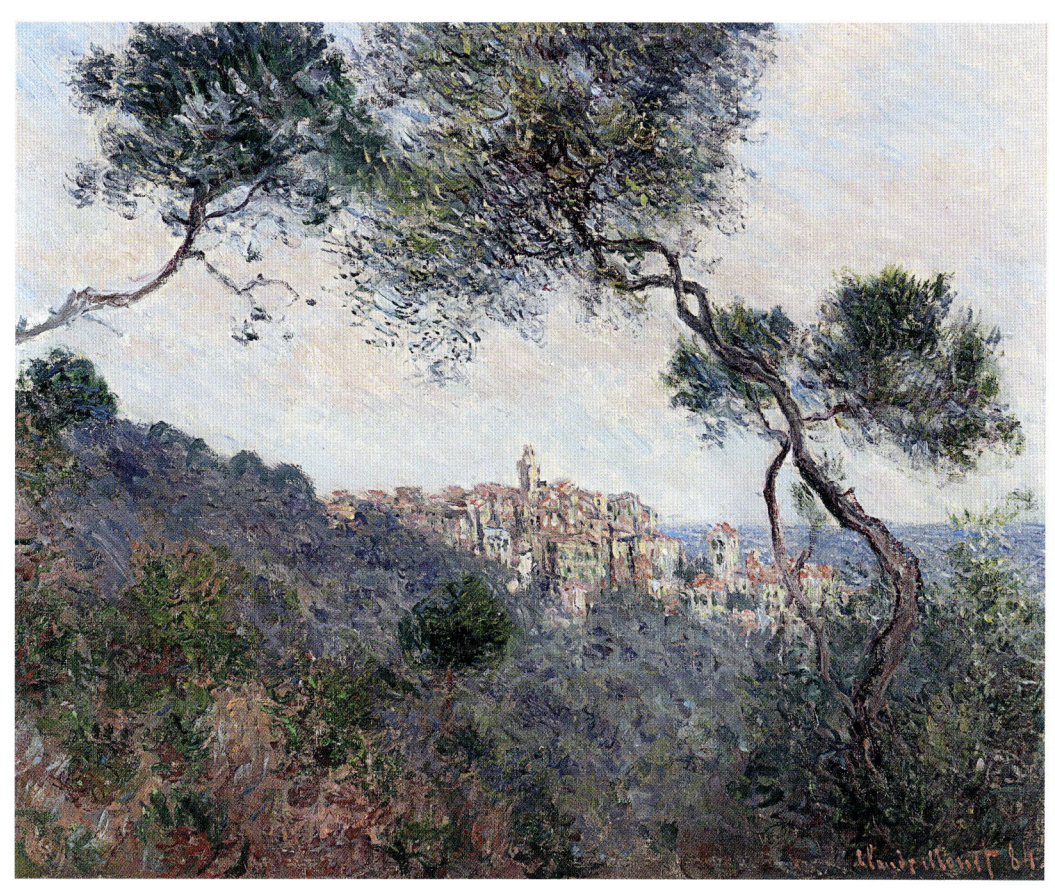

The Manneporte (Étretat), 1886

Oil on canvas
65.4 × 81.3 cm
The Metropolitan Museum of Art, New York

In 1886 the French writer Guy de Maupassant came across Claude Monet walking along the beach at Étretat in Normandy with children helping to carry his many canvases, all of the same subject, the projecting arched cliff. Later, watching Monet's method of painting, the writer commented: "He took them up [the canvases] and put them aside by turns according to changes in the sky and shadows." This had become Monet's method of painting since the 1870s, creating series of works capturing his subject matter at different times of day. Monet produced multiple canvases depicting the rocky, hollowed-out Étretat projection in 1883, 1885 and 1886. He painted Étretat eighteen times in 1883 alone. It captivated his creative genius.

The Manneporte (Étretat) is a close-up view of the cliff projection; it could be a creature dipping its head in the water to drink. It is said that Monet's inspiration for the composition came from one of his Japanese prints, The Entrance to the Cave at Enoshima Island in Sagami Province, 1853, a colour woodblock print by Utagawa Hiroshige (1797–1858) with strong waves buffeting a craggy cliff in windy weather. Whatever the weather, Monet painted; changing canvases, changing his viewpoint, climbing rock faces to glimpse a different view, to capture the remarkable atmosphere created by this monolithic wonder. Monet loved the place. He lived in Étretat in 1886. It must have been difficult to carry his canvases and painting gear along the windy beach, but he was undeterred. He wrote: "Étretat is becoming more and more amazing. Now is the real moment: the beach with all its fine boats; it is superb, and I am enraged not to be more skillful in rendering all this. I would need two hands and hundreds of canvases."

Since painting early works like The Porte d'Amont, Étretat, ca. 1868–69 (Harvard Art Museums/Fogg Museum, Cambridge, Mass.), with its magnificent sunset, Étretat's rocky crags and sea swirling around them entranced him. Monet managed to produce eighteen views of them in 1883 and more would follow. A painting very different from The Manneporte (Étretat) is Boats on the Beach at Étretat, 1885 (The Art Institute of Chicago). A rough sea, four boats and three huts dominate the picture space. Monet painted it from a window of the Hôtel Blanquet while waiting for the weather to change.

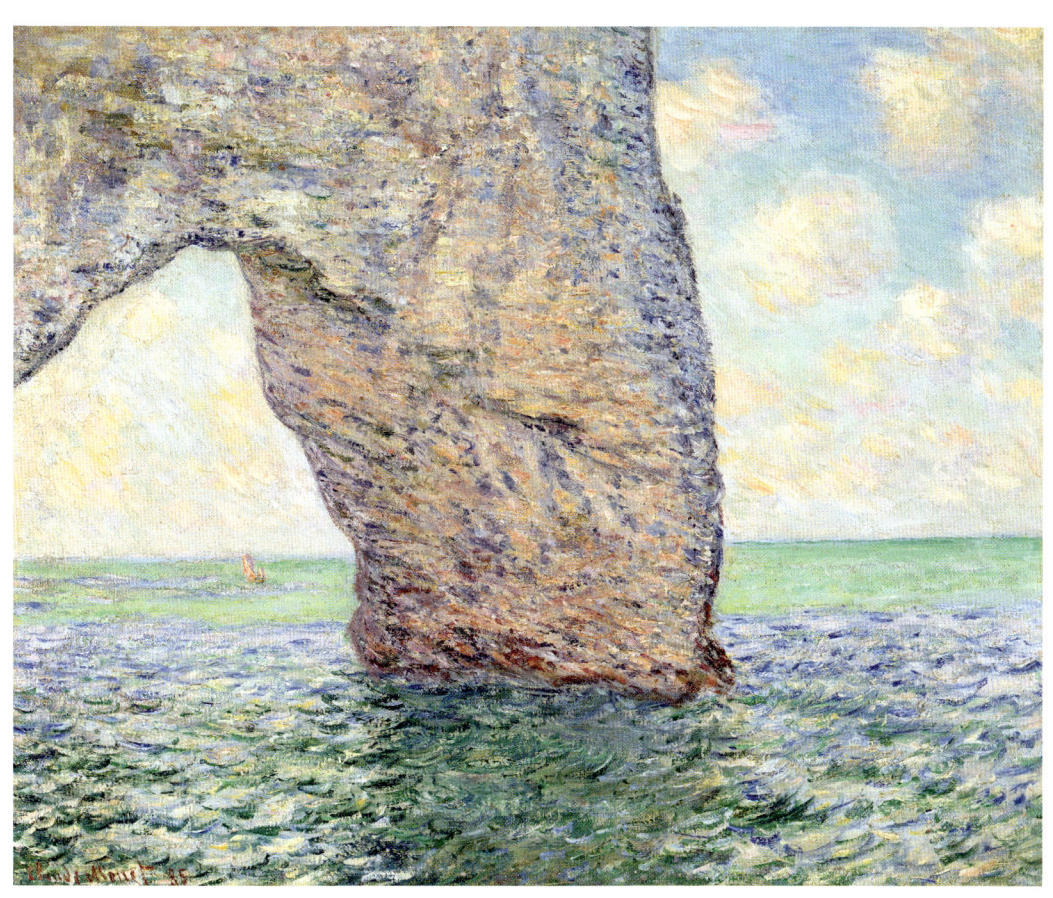

Antibes, 1888

Oil on canvas
65.5 × 92,4 cm
The Courtauld Gallery, London

From January to May 1888 Monet stayed in Antibes, in the Alpes-Maritime region
in the south of France. Antibes was founded in the fourth century B.C. as a Greek
colony, becoming a walled, fortified town in later centuries. Situated between
Cannes and Nice and with a population of around 6,700, it was a haven for artists
in Monet's time. Painters delighted in the intense sunlight.
Monet had fled the colder climate of Giverny and Paris for the warm south – although
January and February could bring changeable weather – planning to stay until the
months of extreme heat approached. He stayed at a boarding house popular with
artists, the Château de la Pinède. In his usual manner he scouted the region for
suitable motifs, exploring the coastline east toward Monte Carlo.
During his stay he created thirty-nine paintings, of which *Antibes* is one of a series
focusing on the area's umbrella and stone pine trees. Looking to the southwest,
he framed his view with a single pine tree with its rich green needles, blown by a
warm wind in front of the sparkling waters of the Mediterranean. In the distance the
mountains of the Esterel extend across the entire canvas. Rich browns, blues and
greens complemented by warm pinks and orange tones convey the warmth of the
sun on the shore. The mountain range is rendered in alternating strokes of pink and
blue, though he insisted that to do justice to the view he would need "a palette of
diamonds and jewels."
On his return home this painting and others in the series were bought by the
art dealers Boussod and Valadon, where his friend and admirer Theo van Gogh
(Vincent's younger brother) was employed.

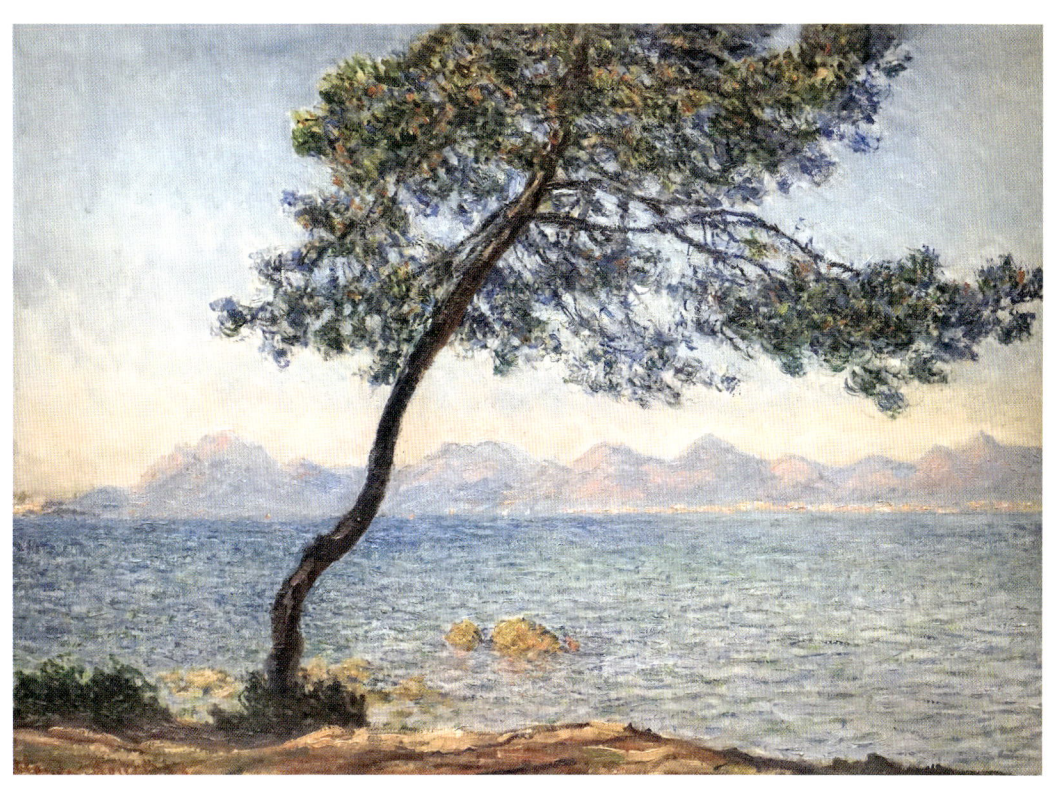

Grainstack in the Sunlight, Snow Effect, 1891

Oil on canvas
65 × 100 cm
Hasso Plattner Collection

A field of haystacks (grainstacks) close to Monet's house in Giverny was the inspiration for a series of works featuring the stacks – in groups, pairs or singly – with houses beyond at different times of day and under different weather conditions. In 1890/91 he made thirty paintings of this scene.

For this composition Monet chose a single haystack with houses and trees in the distance. He used a palette of red lake, vermilion, ultramarine blue, cadmium yellow, viridian and lead white. The deeper colours of the haystack contrast with the warm oranges, pinks and yellows layering the sky. It is reflected in the ice-white snow gently melting in the sun, rendered in pale blues, pale purple and soft lavenders and pinks. Behind the haystack we glimpse roofs of houses and some trees. The hills in the distance recede toward the right.

While working on this series he wrote to a friend, the art critic Gustave Geoffroy, explaining what he was up to: "I am working very hard, struggling with a series of different effects (haystacks), but at this season the sun sets so fast I cannot follow it. … The more I continue, the more I see that a great deal of work is necessary in order to succeed in rendering what I seek." He told Geoffroy that what he was after was "instantaneity," capturing one moment of light before it disappeared to change the scene before him.

Monet's haystack series was a great success. This painting was sold to his dealer Paul Durand-Ruel in May 1891. In the same month the Durand-Ruel gallery presented the *Exposition d'oeuvres recentes de Cl. Monet*, in which fifteen of twenty-two paintings displayed were from this series.

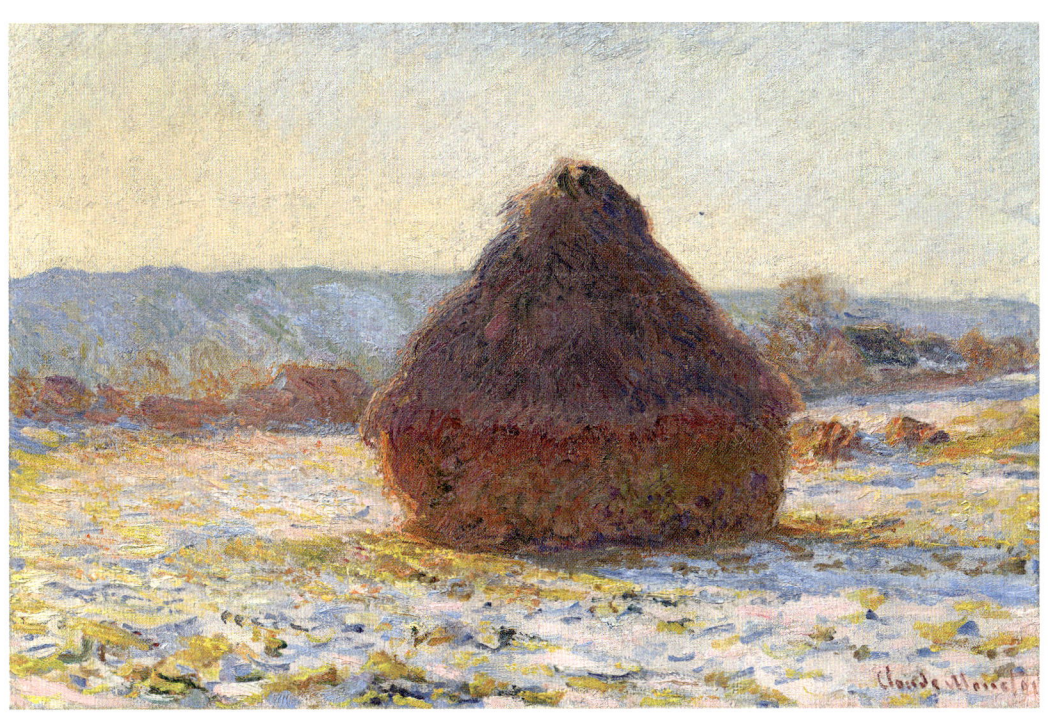

Poplars in the Sun, 1891

Oil on canvas
93 × 73.5 cm
National Museum of Western Art, Tokyo

Painted in the Spring of 1891, *Poplars in the Sun*, exhibited in 1892 as *Les Trois Arbres, Été* (*The Three Trees, Summer*), is one of twenty-four Monet paintings depicting tall poplars along the banks of river Epte, close to Monet's house in Giverny. He painted the trees from various viewpoints at different times of the day and in different seasons, capturing their changing foliage, the sunlight on their leaves and the ambient mood, their height lending a sense of elegance to the beauty of the landscape. His time was limited, as the trees were destined to be cut down. The farmer-owner had sold them for timber, but delayed the felling until Monet had completed his cycle of the seasons. The vantage point is low, at water level, for Monet painted from a rowboat on the river. The boat was fitted out with slots to hold several canvases on which he would work simultaneously, perhaps taking out one for only minutes at a time in order to capture a specific light effect or changing cloud formations. The boat was apparently not suitable for the prolonged time he spent in it, for in September 1891 Monet wrote to his artist friend Gustave Caillebotte asking to borrow his boat. "Your boat would be a big help to me just now. I'm painting a lot of pictures on the river Epte and am very uncomfortable in my Norwegian rowing boat. If you don't really need it, send it to me either by steamer to Vernon or Port-Villez, or by rail. Rail would be most practical. Drop me a line anyway."
Monet's confidence that the poplar paintings would sell was perfectly justified. Even before Durand-Ruel exhibited fifteen of them in March 1892 Monet had sold six to the gallerist and six more were sold through Durand-Ruel's New York gallery. Additional sales resulted from a show of the works at the gallery Boussod and Valadon et Cie. With his growing reputation Monet chose to work with more than one dealer, thereby increasing the chances of sales in Europe and America.

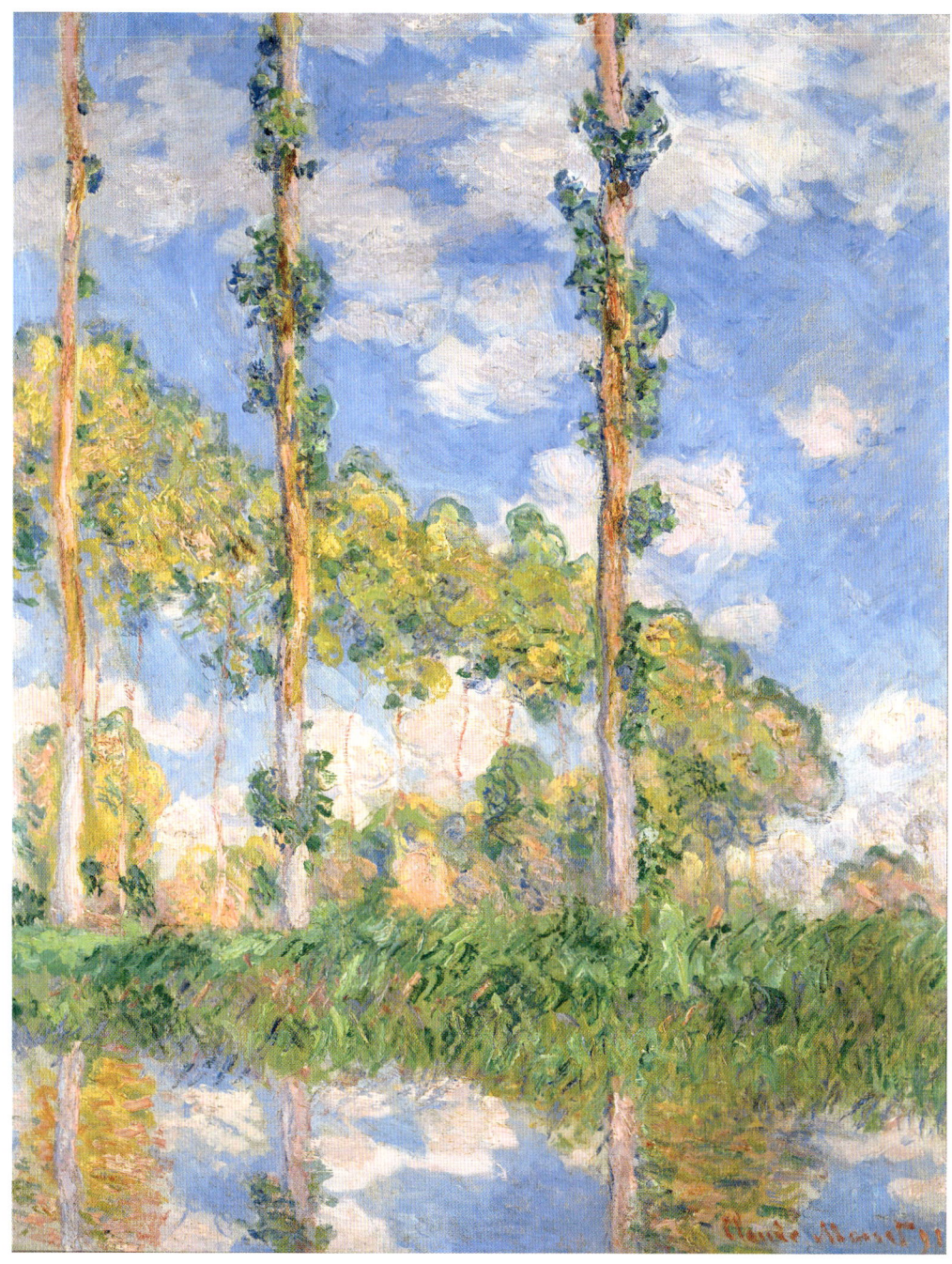

Rouen Cathedral, West Façade, Sunlight, 1894

Oil on canvas
100.1 × 65.8 cm
National Gallery of Art, Washington, Chester Dale Collection

Monet chose two locations in which to paint his views of the façade of Rouen cathedral. Their angles depended on where he could rent spaces in the buildings opposite. One was a millinery shop at 23 Place de la Cathedrale – a beautiful building that now houses the Rouen tourist office. He worked from a second-floor room overlooking the cathedral square that he shared with a screened-off changing room. There he was very close to the west façade, and it would have been difficult to survey the whole cathedral. The other spot was an empty apartment a short distance away at the corner of rue du Gros Horloge and rue Grand-Point. He took this again on his return in February–April 1893 as well as another in rue Grand-Point that provided him with a wider view of the façade. Renting different rooms gave him the opportunity to paint the façade at different times of day from different angles.

Painting such a vast building from behind a window was not ideal. Monet limited his view to its west front, zooming in on the portal and cutting off the towers. The structure's great height is indicated by the three small figures on the left outside the cathedral door. Monet again worked on a series of canvases, switching from one to another as the light and weather changed. Sunlight swept the façade after midday, moving from right to left. This view would have been painted between noon and two on days when the sun shone.

In a letter to his wife Alice from 31 March 1892 Monet wrote of his concern that the good weather was delaying the completion of his "grey weather" paintings. His goal was to paint the *effet* (effect) of what he was seeing. His brushstrokes are thickly textured, highlighting the stone while retaining a sense of the building's majesty.

The following year Monet continued to agonise over his chosen subject, writing to Alice on 22 February: "What terrible unsettled weather! I carry on regardless without a break. … Dear God, this cursed cathedral is hard to do…it will come in the end with a hard struggle. I'm glad I decided to come back."

Monet completed his series of more than thirty paintings of Rouen cathedral in his studio in Giverny in 1894. He exhibited twenty of the works with great success at Durand-Ruel's Paris gallery in 1895.

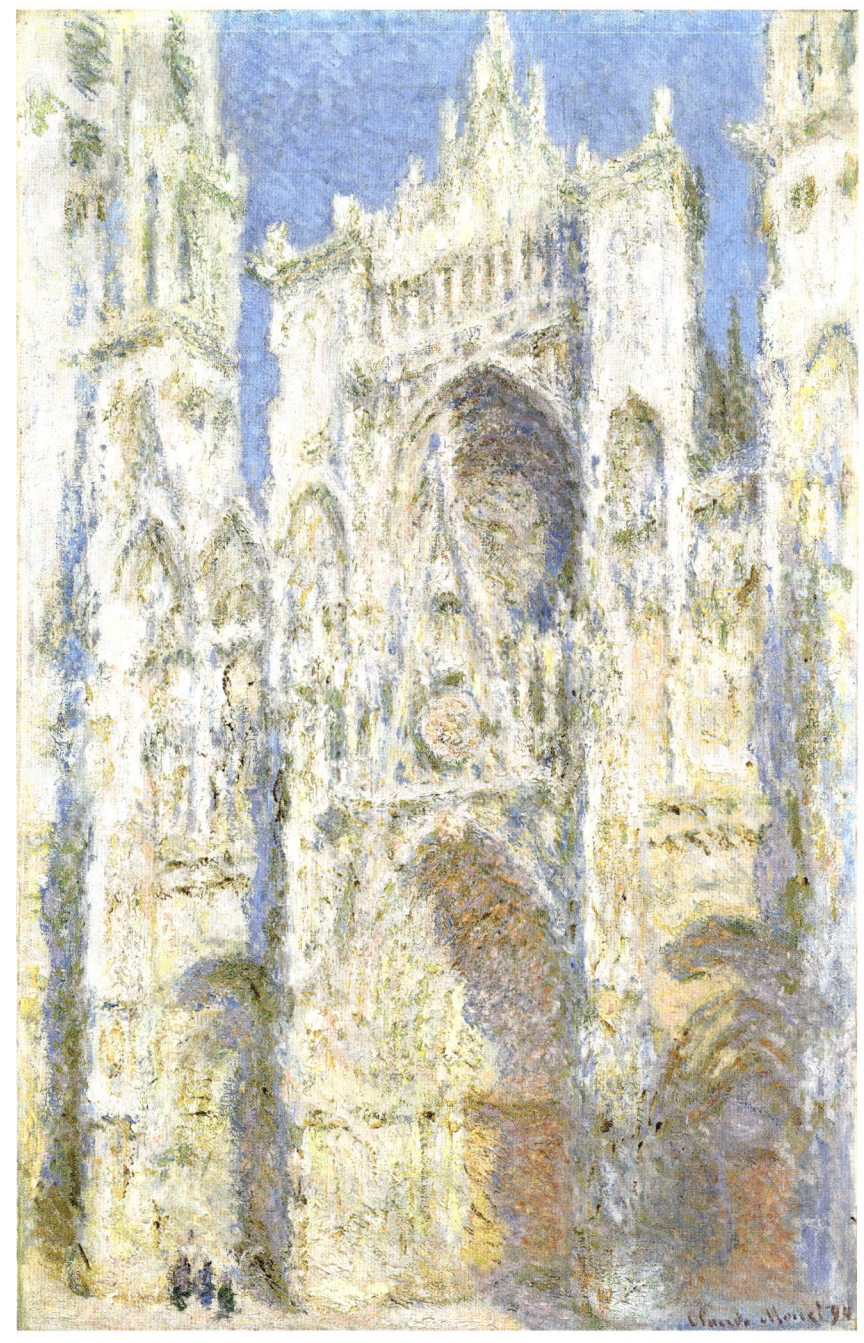

Norwegian Landscape, Blue Houses, 1895

Oil on canvas
61 × 84 cm
Musée Marmottan Monet, Paris

After spending the spring of 1892 and 1893 in Rouen painting his series on the cathedral, then completing the works in Giverny in 1894, in early 1895 he travelled to Christiania, Norway (now Oslo), where his stepson Jacques Hoschedé was living with his Norwegian wife. He stayed for two months, travelling around and sketching and painting. The brilliance of sunlight on the snow drifts captured his imagination. Venturing out in horse-drawn sleighs, he was able to reach stunning locations where at times he worked outdoors in temperatures well below zero. He wrote to a friend that at times he was immersed in snow with his beard full of icy stalactites. Paintings like the present one capture the brilliance of sun on snow, the wintry beauty of houses, waterways and snowdrifts in and around Christiania.

After familiarising himself with that area he travelled west to Björnegaard, where he stayed in a rented room. The town had an artists' colony. The strikingly beautiful landscapes of pure white, virgin snow exaggerated the colours of the houses and buildings, as one sees in his *Red Houses at Björnegaard, Norway* (1895, Musée Marmottan Monet, Paris). Red walls accentuate the houses' white snow-covered low roofs and patches of pale blue on the snow drifts mirror the rich blue of the sky. During his stay he painted stunning views of Sandvika, a town on the Sandvika river, capturing the snow-covered houses in a series of paintings featuring the picturesque Lokke bridge spanning the river. While painting the bridge he possibly recalled his copy of Utagawa Hiroshige's print *Meguro Drum Bridge and Sunset Hill, No. 111*. Travelling around Sandvika, Monet painted a series featuring the Christiania (Oslo) Fjord, the water surrounded by snow-covered hills, and finally thirteen views of the colossal Mount Kolsås, near Christiania. It reminded him of views of Japan's Mount Fuji. Six were exhibited in a Durand-Ruel exhibition that same year. Once the snow began to melt he planned his return to Giverny, but not before receiving an impromptu visit by Prince Eugen of Sweden and Norway, a commendable painter and an admirer of Monet's work. Monet finally left for France on 1 April.

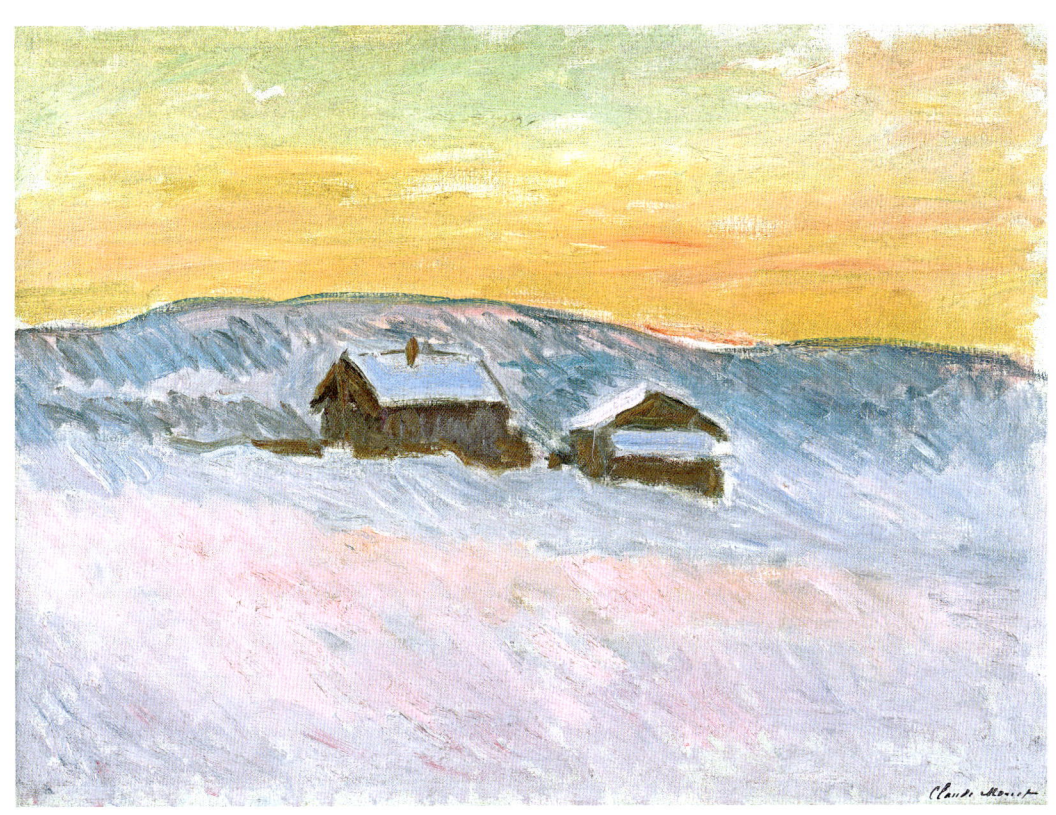

The Japanese Footbridge, 1899

Oil on canvas
81.3 × 101.6 cm
National Gallery of Art, Washington, Gift of Victoria Nebeker Coberly, in memory
of her son John W. Mudd, and Walter H. and Leonore Annenberg

In 1893, after having purchased the Giverny house three years before, Monet also
bought a piece of boggy wetland across the road, as he wanted to expand his
garden. He planned to create a large pond with flowing water. To do so he applied
to the local council for permission to divert a tributary of the river Epte across his
new property. Permission was granted and he set about designing a Japanese-
inspired water garden. He planted the pond with the white water lilies seen in
this painting, and added the beechwood "Japanese" footbridge made by a local
craftsman. It was painted in a greenish-blue, the colour of some of the bridges in
Japanese prints. Later paintings show wisteria growing above the bridge. He may
have been inspired by his copy of Hiroshige's *Wisteria at Kameido Tenjin Shrine,*
which pictures an arch over the bridge for wisteria to trail on. Twelve works from
this period include the Japanese bridge and the water below. The bridge with
its reflection in the water would ultimately appear in a full forty-five paintings.
Monet was an avid collector of Japanese prints, and more than two hundred were
hung throughout his house. He admired their simple composition and subject
matter, their sense of serenity. His water-lily paintings have the same sense of place
and atmosphere. He wanted to paint the breeze and he nearly managed to in
this tranquil water setting. In a later series the depiction of the bridge is almost
abstract; it is simply glimpsed beneath the vivid red and yellow brushstrokes, as in
The Japanese Bridge, 1918 (Musée Marmottan Monet, Paris). In *The Japanese Bridge,*
ca. 1918–24 (Fondation Beyeler, Basel), it is again nearly hidden by the deep blue-
greens of the water and foliage. In his late paintings Monet concentrated exclusively
on the water lilies in the pond and the reflections in the water.

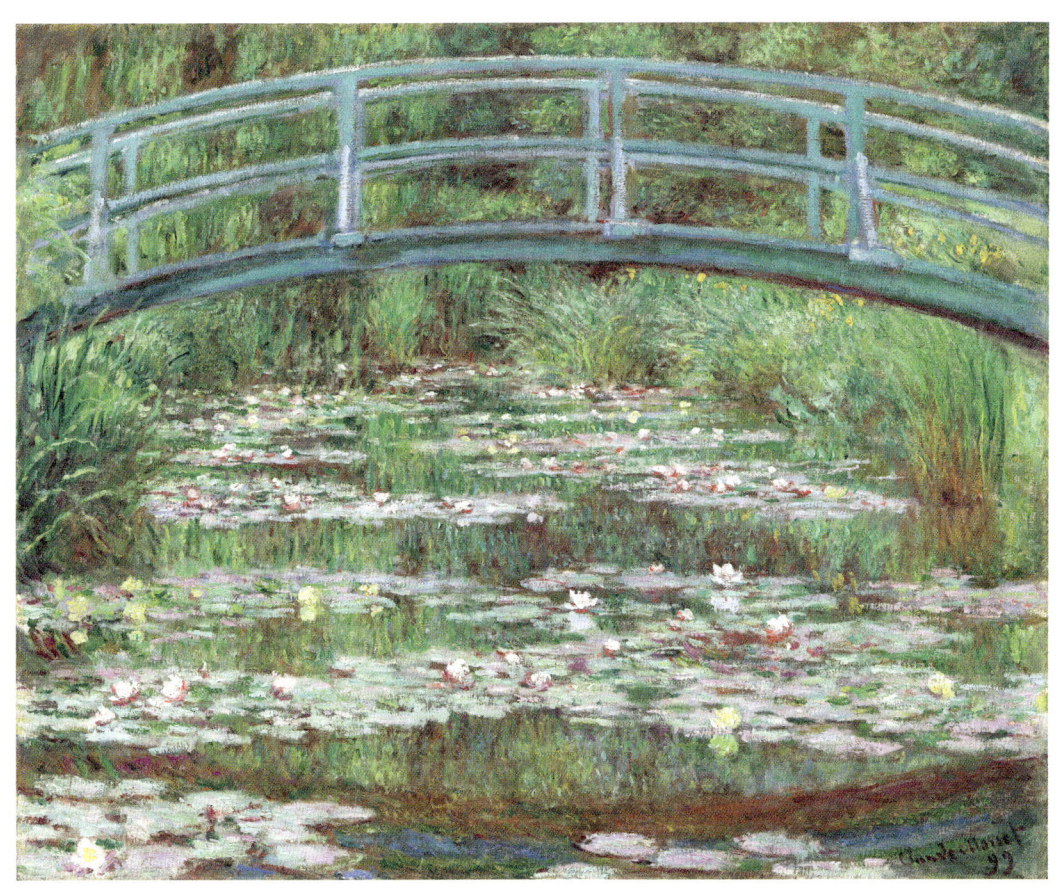

The Artist's Garden at Giverny, 1900

Oil on canvas
81.6 × 92.6 cm
Musée d'Orsay, Paris

Claude Monet loved his gardens wherever he lived and carefully planned how each one should look. The one in Giverny must have been a paradise. A letter to his gardener from February 1900 shows that his plans for the coming season were well underway. His planting scheme assured that the garden would not only be pleasant to look at, sit in and enjoy but also to paint. He wrote: "Sowing around 300 pots Poppies – 60 sweet peas – around 60 pots white Agrimony – 30 yellow Agrimony – Blue sage – Blue Water lilies in beds (greenhouse) – Dahlias – Iris Kaempferi. From the 15th to 25th, lay the dahlias down to root; plant those with shoots before I get back. ... Don't delay work on tarring the planks and plant the *Helianthus latiflorus* in good clumps right away."

Monet's planting scheme is evident in this canvas painted that same year. Instead of placing one or two clumps here and there he preferred densely planted beds filled with rich colour. His instructions to his gardener were detailed: "Keep a close eye on the gloxinia," and "get down to pruning: rose trees not too long." Monet could see in his mind's eye the layout of his extensive gardens and knew exactly where he wanted plants placed. His garden enthralled everyone who came to visit. Here we see the central path leading back to Monet's house. To the left and right of it are dense plantings of purple irises and other plants with purple blooms, all in full-flower. Dappled sun falls on the flower beds, filtering through the red spruce trees standing tall in the background. The trees were later removed. Other paintings of this part of the garden feature a similar but different view, as in *The Main Path at Giverny*, 1902 (Österreichische Galerie Belvedere, Vienna). He never produced exactly the same composition, altering each representation slightly by viewpoint or angle. Monet was quoted as saying that he was only good at two things: painting and gardening. The proof of this is seen in his masterful depictions of his gardens at Giverny.

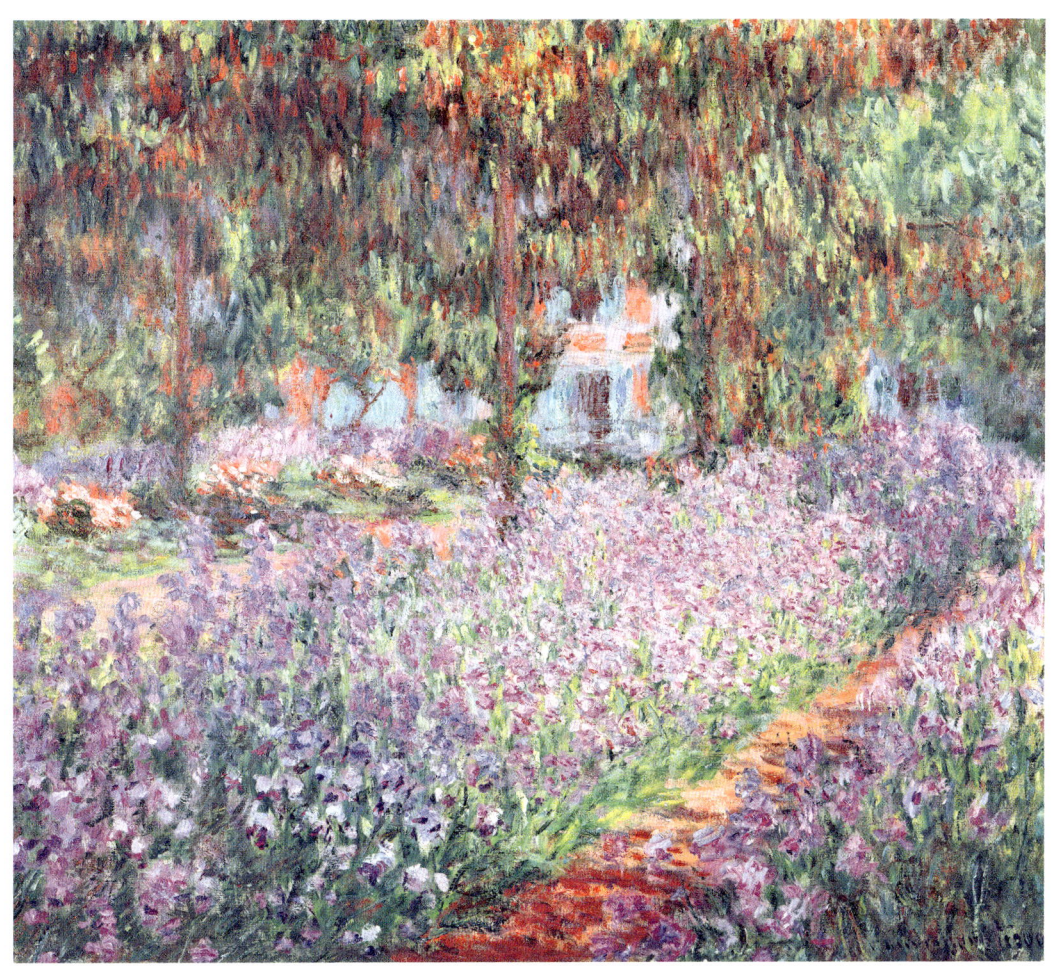

Waterloo Bridge, Grey Weather, 1900

Oil on canvas
65.4 × 92.6 cm
The Art Institute of Chicago, Gift of Mrs. Mortimer B. Harris

"Without the fog," Monet said, "London wouldn't be a beautiful city. It's the fog that gives it its magnificent breadth. Its regular and massive blocks become grandiose within that mysterious cloak." In wintry weather, as pictured in this view of Waterloo Bridge, London fogs were often so poisonous that they asphyxiated cattle in nearby Smithfield Market and blighted the health of Londoners living and working in the city. In autumn and winter the "pea-souper" fogs created a darkness that only lifted around 10 a.m. if the sun shone. This was what Monet had come to London to paint. He loved how the combination of sunlight, fog and belching factory smoke created atmospheric effects in the sky and on the water. He enjoyed depicting what he described as "some fog effects." Monet wrote to his wife Alice: "It has to be said that this climate is so idiosyncratic; you wouldn't believe the amazing effects I have seen in the nearly two months that I have been constantly looking at this river Thames." For Monet London's Monday-to-Saturday working week was most favourable, when factory chimneys were pouring out the smoke just visible through fog in another view of this scene with a little more sunshine in a brighter sky and more traffic, *Waterloo Bridge, Overcast Weather*, 1900 (Hugh Lane Gallery, Dublin). Sundays, when factories were idle, pollution was reduced, and there was less traffic, were not so appealing. Monet spent his time drawing and making starts of paintings. He went home with more than a hundred unfinished canvases, which he completed in his Giverny studio. Many paintings, like *Charing Cross Bridge. Smoke in the Fog; Impression*, 1902 (Musée Marmottan Monet, Paris), have the words "fog" or "smoke" or "effect of fog" in their titles. His depictions of the Houses of Parliament, painted from the roof of St Thomas' hospital on the South Bank, are large square canvases. *The Houses of Parliament, Sunset*, 1904 (Kunstmuseum, Krefeld, Kaiser Wilhelm Museum), was the first from the series to enter a public collection, purchased by the Kaiser Wilhelm Museum in 1907. Both of the above were among the thirty-seven paintings exhibited in Paris in 1904 as *Views of the Thames in London*. The show was highly praised and many of the paintings were sold. Monet had planned to repeat the exhibition in London the following year but the success of the Paris show had left him with only a few canvases to exhibit and the new owners were unwilling to part with others.

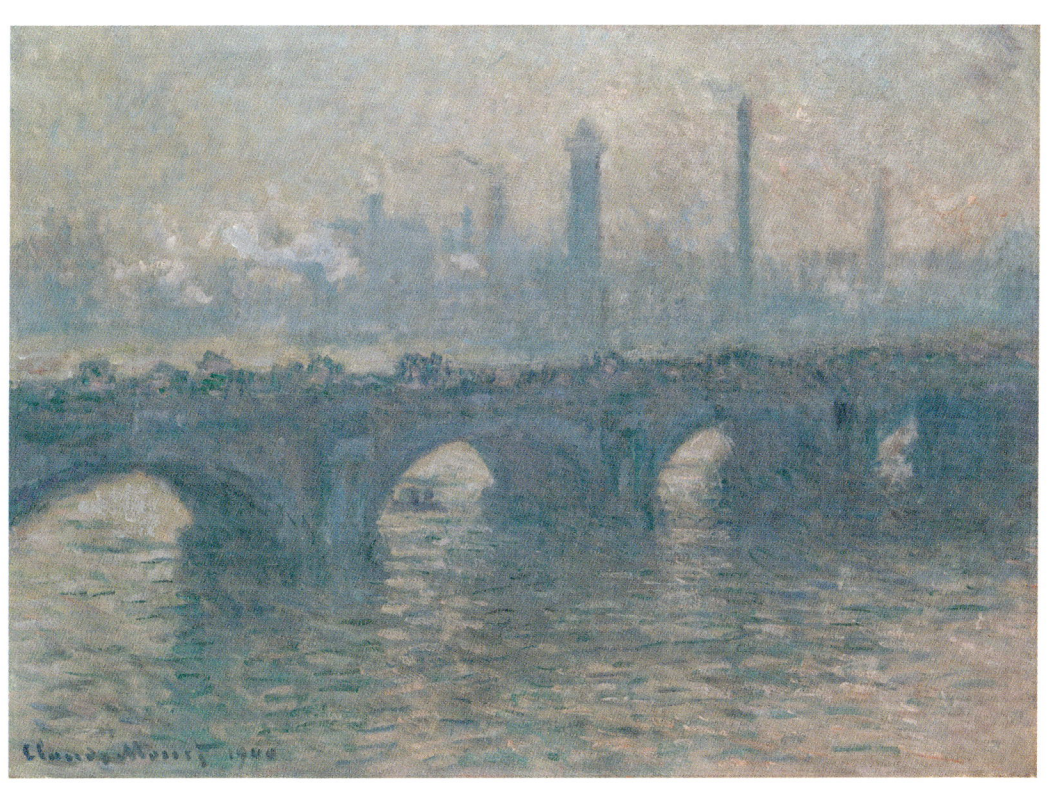

Houses of Parliament, London, Sun Breaking Through the Fog, 1904

Oil on canvas
81.5 × 92.5 cm
Musée d'Orsay, Paris

For the Houses of Parliament paintings Monet chose large, square canvases that he must have had custom made. He painted them from a private terrace on the top floor of St Thomas' Hospital across the river. He had gained permission to use this facility on his earlier visit in 1900. In his depictions of Parliament he focused on the Victoria Tower, preferring to paint the view in the late afternoon with the sun setting behind the complex. As he often did, he wrote to his wife Alice about his progress. Of this painting he wrote: "Here, very fine weather today and, a rare thing, sunshine, and, as I thought, the sun is already setting very far from the place that I had dreamed of having it set in a huge ball of fire behind Parliament." Although Monet did not acknowledge J.M.W. Turner's use of a rising or setting sun as a focal point, there are similarities between Monet's depiction and Turner's 1838 *Fighting Temeraire* (1839, The National Gallery, London), where the sun is seen setting behind the iron-hulled ship being towed to its final berth to be scrapped.

Monet's days in London did not always go according to plan. A letter to his wife Alice written at noon on 19 March 1900 found him in utter despair after finding when he got up that the roofs of buildings were covered in snow. The day's chill and wraparound fog with no sun meant the snow remained. Monet had fifteen canvases in progress none with snow in them. The letter poured out his frustration, but before he finished it he reported that there was brilliant sunshine outside. The snow would melt but he had packed away the canvases in crates.

Looking back to his paintings of the Thames from thirty years before, those of 1900 and 1904 clearly feature atmosphere over architecture. *The Thames, London*, 1871 (National Museum Wales) could be compared to Monet's later paintings of Venice in 1908; the buildings and many boats on the river are clearly defined, the latter with a momentary sense of movement. By 1900 his emphasis was on the mood and the weather.

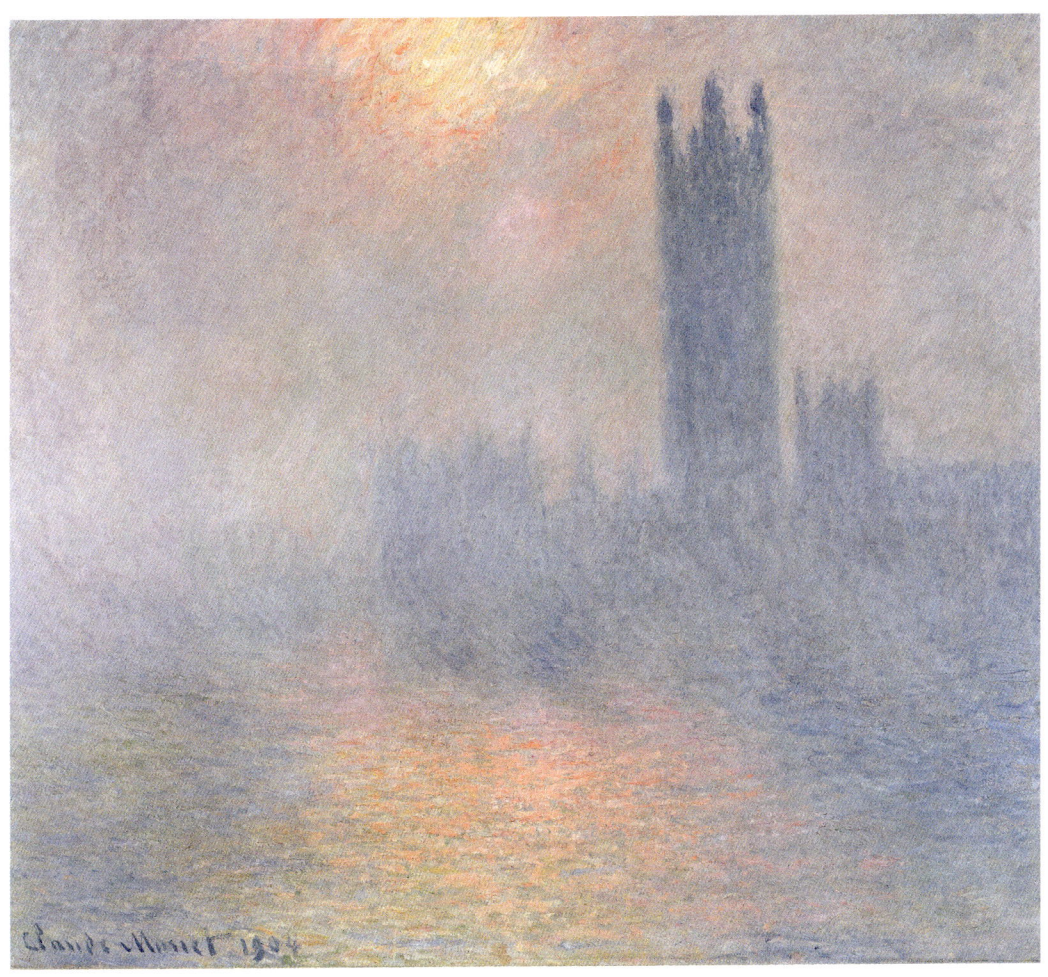

The Palazzo Contarini, 1908

Oil on canvas
73 × 92 cm
Hasso Plattner Collection

From late September to December 1908 Monet took a holiday in Venice with
his wife Alice. A contemporary photograph shows them relaxing, feeding the
pigeons in St Mark's Square. A pigeon is sitting on Monet's head. He had planned
for the visit to take place after his preparation of a major exhibition of his latest
series of paintings of water lilies at Giverny. He was drained from the planning
and the selection of works to be shown. When Durand-Ruel visited Giverny to
help in March 1908, Monet decided to add another series to the show, which
delayed the opening until 1909, so instead he took the trip to Venice with Alice.
He loved Venice and regretted not visiting it sooner. Monet took his painting
equipment and set about painting famous Venetian landmarks: the Doge's
Palace, the Grand Canal, Palazzo Dario, Palazzo da Mula, San Giorgio Maggiore,
the Palazzo Contarini and more, mostly observed from the water. Édouard Manet
once remarked that Monet was the "Raphael of water," and here he was in La
Serenissima, a breathtaking city built in a lagoon. Two of his residences in the
city helped determine his motifs. From late September to mid October the
couple were private guests at the Palazzo Barbaro on the Grand Canal. It was
from the Palazzo Barbaro that Monet painted *The Palazzo Contarini*. They then
moved to the Hotel Grand Britannia, also on the north bank of the Grand Canal in
the heart of Venice. Each day he hired a gondola and set out with Alice and his
painting equipment to paint from the water.
The Palazzo Contarini was built around 1499 for the wealthy Contarini family.
Its architecture is a mix of Gothic, Renaissance and Moorish styles. Its beautiful
design includes an external spiral staircase at the rear. Monet's atmospheric
depiction of the remarkable building shows the jewel-like, deep blue water
lapping at its entrance. His Venetian paintings were exhibited at the Bernheim-
Jeune gallery in Paris in 1912, under the title *Venise*. This painting was bought
from Monet by Bernheim-Jeune and Durand-Ruel in May 1912.

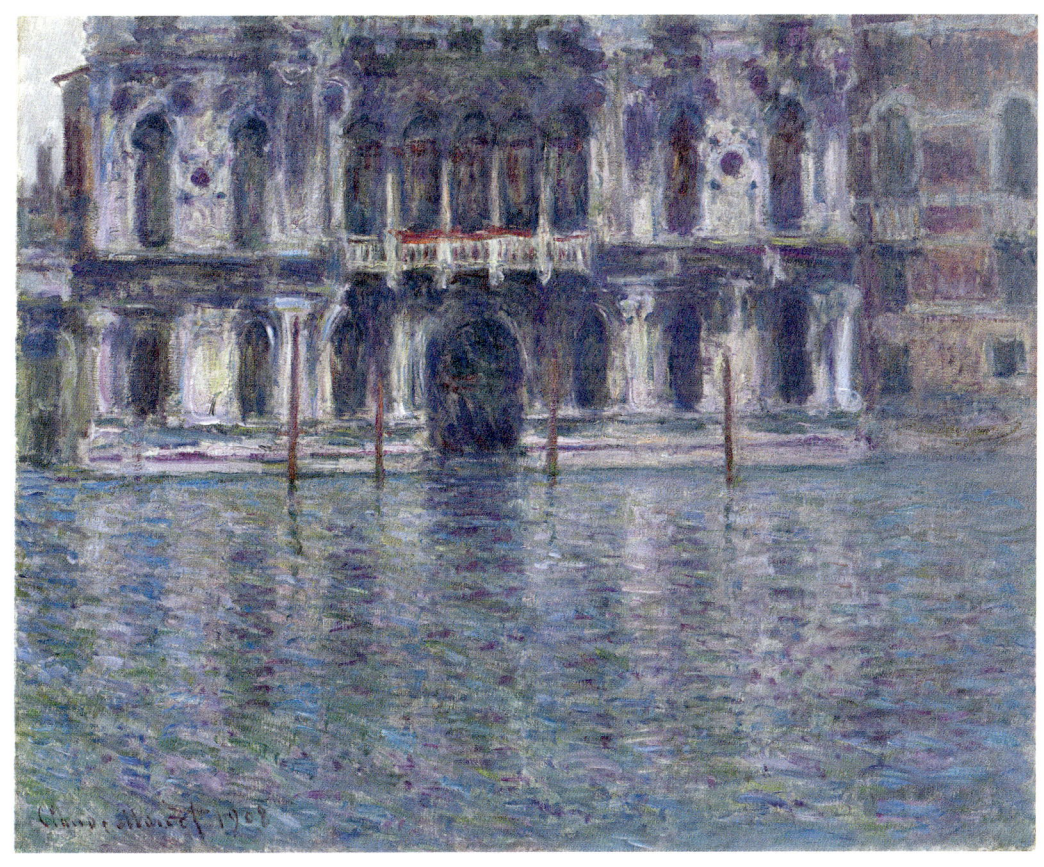

The Water-Lily Pond in the Evening, 1914–22

Oil on canvas
Two panels, each 200 × 300 cm
Kunsthaus Zürich

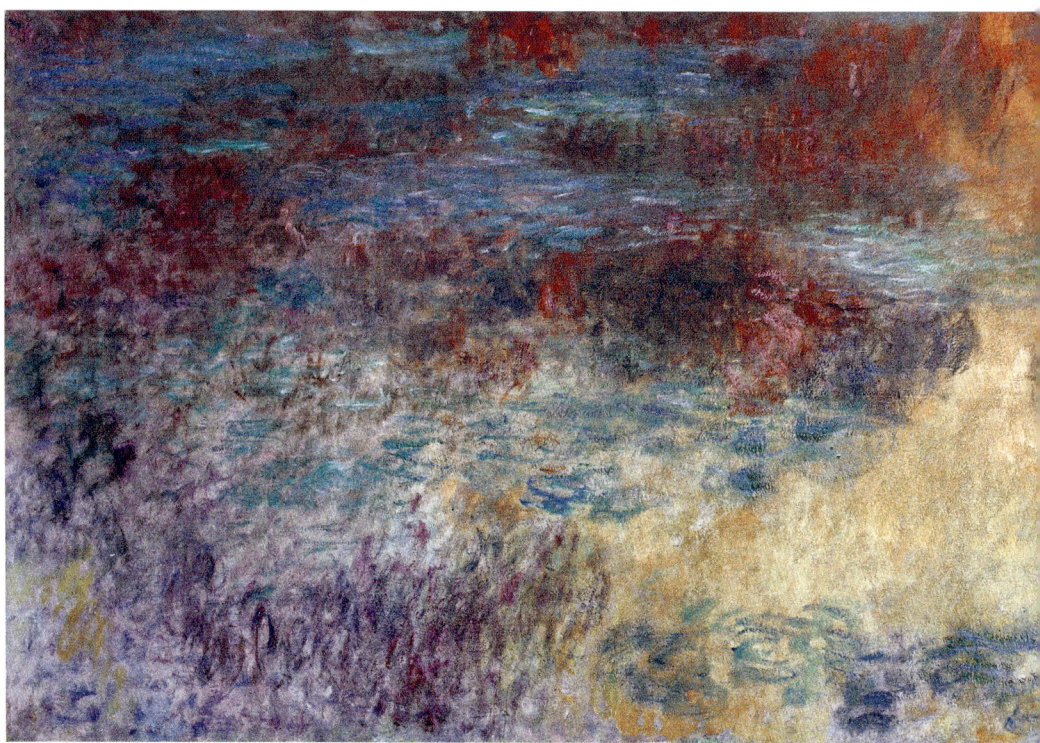

In May 1909 Monet exhibited forty-eight water-lily paintings at Durand-Ruel's in Paris. The show was a great success, praised by collectors, art critics and an enthusiastic public. From 1902 to 1908 Monet had first focused on the pond, the willows and the irises and agapanthus growing at its edges, but as he progressed he gradually abandoned the extraneous enhancements around the water to concentrate on the water itself and the water lilies in it. In 1909 he discovered that his wife Alice was terminally ill. After their return from Venice in 1908 it was found that she was suffering from spinal leukaemia. Her death on 18 May 1911 devastated the painter, and it would be years before he was able to work again. A second family death followed in 1914; at only forty-six his beloved son Jean died a painful death, possibly from syphilis. Blanche Hoschedé Monet, Jean's widow and Monet's step-daughter, moved to Giverny permanently, which was a consolation to them both.

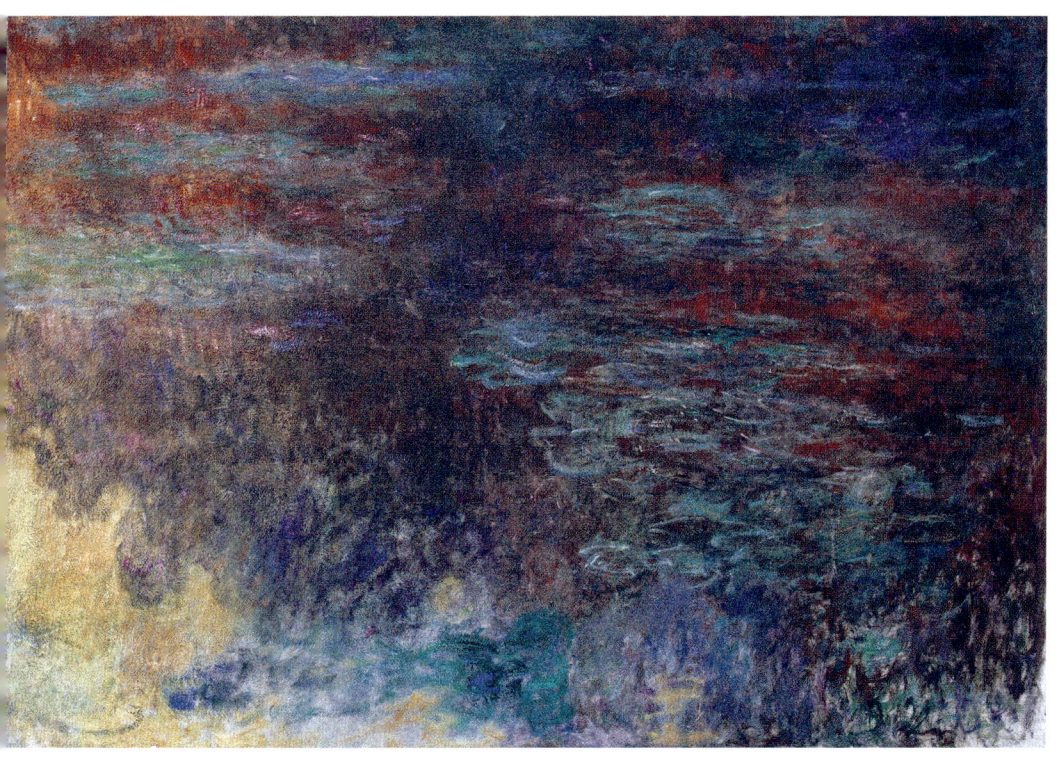

It was not until June 1914 that he felt ready to take up painting again, but soon war in Europe, with fighting at times not far from Giverny, would further depress him, as there was little he could do. His water-lily pond provided him with comfort and a degree of serenity, and he continued to invest in its upkeep. He produced more than 200 paintings that included the plants growing around the pond in this part of the garden – yellow irises, violet-blue agapanthus, red-flowered daylilies given extraordinary depth of colour.

This large diptych started during World War One adds another perspective to his water-lily paintings. Although completed at a later date, it relates to earlier works from 1907 onward that Monet kept. The burnished light at the centre is surrounded by the encroaching darkness. At first glance the painting looks to be an abstraction, with colour replacing reality, but a closer look discovers swathes of lily pads floating in an ethereal, majestic atmosphere.

FURTHER READING

Baudelaire, Charles, *The Painter of Modern Life and Other Essays*, Phaidon 1995.

Callen, Anthea, *The Art of Impressionism: Painting Technique & the Making of Modernity*, Yale University Press 2000.

Groom, Gloria (ed.), *Impressionism, Fashion & Modernity*, Yale University Press, New Haven and London, 2012.

Patry, Sylvie (ed.), *Inventing Impressionism: Paul Durand-Ruel and the Modern Art Market*, National Gallery, London, 2015.

Thomson, Richard, *Monet and Architecture*, National Gallery, London, 2018.

Wildenstein, Daniel. *Monet or The Triumph of Impressionism*, vol. 1, Wildenstein Institute, Taschen, 1996.

Wildenstein, Daniel. *Monet: Catalogue Raisonné*, vols. 2–4, Wildenstein Institute, Taschen, 1996.

Wullschläger, Jackie. *Monet: The Restless Vision*, Knopf 2024.

Monet: The Early Years, exh. cat. Kimbell Art Museum, Fort Worth, Yale University Press 2017.

Monet: The Late Years, exh. cat. Kimbell Art Museum, Fort Worth, Yale University Press 2019.

PHOTO CREDITS